D0424024

The Language of Mystery

EDWARD ROBINSON

The Language
of Mystery

SCM PRESS

London

TRINITY PRESS INTERNATIONAL

Philadelphia

First published 1987
Second impression 1989

Copyright © Edward Robinson 1987

SCM Press   Trinity Press International
26–30 Tottenham Road   3725 Chestnut Street
London N1 4BZ   Philadelphia, Pa. 19104

All rights reserved. No part of this publication may be
reproduced, stored in a retrieval system, or transmitted,
in any form or by any means, electronic, mechanical,
photocopying, recording or otherwise, without the prior
permission of the publishers, SCM Press and Trinity
Press International.

British Library Cataloguing in Publication Data

Robinson, Edward, 1921–
    The language of mystery.
    1. Imagination—Religious aspects—
    Christianity
    I. Title
    233'.5   BR115.16

    ISBN 0-334-02138-3

Library of Congress Cataloging-in-Publication Data

Robinson, Edward, 1921–
    The language of mystery/Edward Robinson.
        p.   cm.
    ISBN 0-334-02138-3: $8.95
    1. Imagination—Religious aspects—Christianity.
    2. Mystery.
    I. Title.
    BR115. I6R56   1989
    246—dc20   89-5021

Phototypeset at The Spartan Press Ltd, Lymington, Hants
and printed in Great Britain by
Richard Clay Ltd, Bungay, Suffolk

CONTENTS

Preface by Bishop John V. Taylor   vii

Introduction   1

1   Mystery and Imagination   5

2   Imagination and Fantasy   15

3   Tradition and the Work of Art   29

4   Art and its Enemies   42

5   Symbol, Sign and Sacrament   52

6   Kitsch in Art and Ritual   60

7   The Mystery of Creation   70

8   Theology and Childhood   78

9   Personal Postscript   85

   Notes   93

PREFACE
by Bishop John V. Taylor

I believe this is the book for which many of us have been waiting. It brings together in a coherent form questions and notions that have been fascinating and eluding us for a long time.

Large numbers of thinking, sensitive people have lost faith in institutional religion; this does not mean that faith itself has ebbed away. For them the traditional statements of belief and forms of prayer have become dead, but not their sense of transcendence or their capacity for worship. Their annual participation in Bach's St Matthew Passion may be the most religious experience of the year, and in the work of certain artists they meet and respond to ultimate reality.

This is partly because the currency of words has been debased. There are too many of them today, and their insistent clamour has earned a widespread mistrust. The human spirit reaches out towards meanings that are more than words can say. The language of religion is full of mental concepts and technical terms that are too rigid for the elusive reality of people's experiences of the Divine. Sensing the misfit, they keep such experiences to themselves, feeling disowned by the religious establishment, and so remain isolated and sterile in that potentially most creative area of their being, as Edward Robinson explains in the second chapter of this book.

His theme is creative imagination, which both Blake and Coleridge recognized as the faculty in which humanity and divinity converge. Blake called it 'the Eternal Body of Man', and Coleridge 'a repetition in the finite mind of the eternal act of creation in the infinite I AM'. However one responds to such grand claims, the word still needs elucidation. Edward Robinson makes clear the contrast between imagination and fantasy and the 'art' which derives from each. Fantasy, he perceives, is essentially self-indulgent, imagination self-forgetful. He calls it 'that capacity for conceiving that the world, and our life in it, need not always be the way it is now'. And he shows that this lies behind the common experience of finding that the writing of a letter or the sharing in a conversation sets one free to give birth to an idea that one has never dreamed of before. Yet imagination is not primarily inventiveness, but vision, the gift of seeing what is already there in a new way. 'The tree which moves some to tears of joy,' says Blake, 'is in the Eyes of others only a Green thing that stands in the way.' In the same vein, Robinson quotes Wallace Stevens (and the reference notes in this book are an exhilarating anthology in themselves): 'The wonder and mystery of art, as indeed of religion in the last resort, is the revelation of something wholly "other" by which the inexpressible loneliness of thinking is broken and enriched.'

Robinson is well aware of that loneliness and of its dangers. So, with a realistic concern for the health of society and of the individual artist or visionary, he affirms the necessity of communication and, consequently, of tradition in any truly creative exercise of imagination.

At one point he very deferentially questions the traditional

Christian teaching that imagination, being a natural endowment, can carry us only so far towards a knowledge of God, and must then give place to faith. With all my heart and mind I would declare that he is right. Imagination and faith are the same thing, 'giving substance to our hopes and reality to the unseen'. The whole Bible endorses this, and if believers talked about faith in these terms they would be more widely understood.

INTRODUCTION

Of all those who have helped me by their comments or criticism in the writing of this book I feel I should give first mention to a publisher's reader who gave as her reason for rejecting an earlier draft that it dealt with 'two quite separate areas of human experience'. The implication was that any attempt to bring the two into a single focus would be of limited interest, or could at any rate have no easily identifiable market. That was for her, understandably, the end of the matter. For me, as I would hope for others, it is only the beginning.

That, at least, is where I start: with a situation in which there is indeed an almost complete separation between the world of religion and the world of the contemporary arts. Almost, but not quite complete; there are in fact signs in many quarters today that the need is being felt for a new rapprochement. Such a separation is, after all, only relatively recent. Go back three hundred years and that meeting of heart and mind between the artist and the church that illuminated so much of mediaeval and renaissance Christendom was still not unknown. Go back even further, to the historic roots of our tradition, or to those primal societies that still exist in something like their original form in today's world, and the distinctions we are familiar with between religion and the various arts of the imagination are either unknown or never made explicit; there is the same kind of affinity between the object of worship and the creative forms in which that worship is expressed as there is between the material from which a pot is made and the form into which it is moulded. It may be that there can be no return for us to that happy state of unselfconsciousness. (I shall have more to say later about the recovery of innocence.) Primitivism, as a deliberate attempt to renounce the present with all its complexities, must always be suspect, if only because complexities generally mean responsibilities.

But if we cannot go back to that lost simplicity, what do we have to go forward to? There are an increasing number of men and women today who feel that we cannot just keep on as we are, with religion going one way and the arts another, on paths at best parallel but more often divergent. Having written that, I wonder: who actually are the 'we' I speak of? Are they to be found among the clergy? Among professional artists, writers, musicians? In each group perhaps only a few, though I would hope a significant few. The feeling is far more widespread among those who in the secularized world of today are conscious, no, who are dimly aware, of a spiritual vacuum, of a freedom that has turned out to be self-consuming, like a recurring decimal, without end and so without purpose. They, we, look for a lead, as we have always done, to those who can speak with the authority of personal insight, and what do we find? A near-total breakdown of communication. The insights may still be there, but how are they to be got across? There is no easy answer to this question – or rather there are an infinity of answers. Those who find security in a language sanctified by long usage find they have nothing in common with those for whom the immediacy of personal experience demands unending experimentation with new forms of expression. It is no intention of mine to take sides in this all too often fruitless debate. On the other hand a chasm so wide is not easily bridged.

What I offer, then, is no more than a series of reflections on a problem that can only be looked at first from one side and then from another. So those who approach it from a traditionally religious point of view may find themselves reasonably engaged by, say, Chapters 5 and 8, but less interested in Chapters 4 and 7, while those whose first concern is with the arts may feel more inclined to skip the discussion of such topics as sacrament, dogma or theology. Short of a systematic exposition of the philosophy or psychology of the religious imagination (however that might be defined) the only way to begin to establish some common ground is to appeal to the everyday experience of those who are anxious to find it. I have called the last section a 'personal postscript'; in fact the whole book, as will immediately be evident, is an essentially personal statement, reflecting my own experience, impatience, frustration – but also gratitude: impatience with some institutions and those whose loyalty to them denies life elsewhere, with some reputations which need to be lopped or even felled for new life to grow alongside them or in their place; gratitude to those many individuals whose work has been the starting point of my own, but above all to a tradition which remains an inexhaustible resource to be drawn upon, and so perpetually renewed, by all those whose imagination is open to what it has continually to reveal.

My idea in writing this book has been to present a text that can be read straight through without the constant interruptions of references to notes. The function of these is to show how the argument can be carried further or be illuminated by reading what others have to say. Also, of course, they frequently indicate the sources of my own ideas.

* I *

Mystery and Imagination

All that we do
Is touched with ocean, yet we remain
On the shore of what we know. [1]

That, in Richard Wilbur's words, is the universal human
condition: to live on the edge of an infinity that touches us at
every point, but which we rarely explore. All of our lives
begin and end in mystery, and though we are generally
successful, often for long periods, in finding distractions that
will keep our minds off it, there are few who do not from time
to time find some sense of this mystery encroaching upon
them.

How is that mystery to be spoken of? And how can any
awareness of it be shared or communicated? From the
beginning of recorded history these questions have been
asked, and in very different ways answered, by saints and

sages, philosophers and theologians, poets and artists. Can there still be anything left to be said? And does it make any sense to speak of a language, let alone the language of mystery?

If the answer to this last question is no – there can after all be no finally satisfactory way of speaking of this mystery – perhaps that is all the more reason for not giving up the inquiry. It means that there will always be more to be said. There is a view common to many traditions that silence alone can do justice to the mystery. Even so, that is a silence that is not like other silences; it is a silence that can communicate; it is a quite specific silence.[2] It is also a fact of common observation that many who have been most insistent that what they have experienced has been beyond description have none the less attempted to describe it at great length, and often very successfully.

My purpose here, then, is to suggest that there is indeed a language of mystery. Not one, so as to exclude all others, but a language nevertheless, that in all its diversity has certain recognizable elements: essential elements, it could be said, which distinguish it from other kinds of language; and necessary elements, without which it could not do its particular job. To demonstrate all this would be beyond the scope of so brief an essay as this. Perhaps it could never be established beyond dispute: this is an area where conviction rather than proof is the best that can be hoped for. What I can do is perhaps to leave my readers wondering whether, in the light of their own experience, there may not be something in what I say.

The first and most distinctive element in this language is this: it is essentially a language of the imagination. Imagination may in itself seem too large and indefinable a concept to be used to define a particular type or style of speech or thought. It does after all pervade much of our thinking. Of course no hard and fast line can be drawn between one kind of language and another; there will always be overlaps. Nevertheless in the language of mystery, I hope to show, imagination is essential, whereas in other forms, or at other levels, of language it is not. It may be at work there, but they can get by without it.

Imagination is something that none of us would readily admit to being wholly without. At the same time, it is something we are generally happier to praise in others than claim ourselves. After all, as Shakespeare tells us, it is 'the lunatic, the lover and the poet' who are 'of imagination all compact'. The rest of us, most of the time at least, can manage pretty well without troubling ourselves too much about it. You have got to keep your feet on the ground: no good letting yourself get carried away by flights of fancy. 'It's all imagination', we say, of ideas that seem to have no grounding in the world of 'fact' in which we feel at home. The 'imaginary' is one thing, the 'real' quite another.

Views like this are daily encouraged by a vast amount of popular literature, film and radio programmes. Even when these purport to be realistic they play on our need (or rather desire) to supplement our often drab experience of the 'real' world with the excitement of an 'imaginary' one. Other forms, such as science fiction, are more explicit in the escape they offer; they all too easily reinforce the already common assumption that the only reality is the material world of the here and now, and that any other is 'pure imagination'.

This view of imagination, as I hope to show, is really quite inadequate. It is inadequate not just to some higher philosophical conception of the nature of mind in relation to the universe, but inadequate to our own personal experience; and that not simply of the everyday situations of life but also of those far profounder questions which, as I say, we keep out of sight much of the time but which tend to catch up with us all in the end.

One reason why imagination is often regarded with some suspicion is that it is commonly confused with fantasy. Everyone is of course free to give any meaning they like to these words, and it is no purpose of mine to lay down how they should or should not be used. It is however possible to show that there are two genuinely different activities which may be at work here, even if they often overlap, and that our lives will be much the poorer if we do not recognize this, whatever names we finally decide to give them. Or one can talk of a single faculty that can be put to two different uses. What is this faculty?

Fundamentally, what appears to distinguish us humans from all other species is the ability to conceive of things being different from the way they are. All other animals seem to be programmed to carry on much as they always have. So they have no history, no technology. They are subject to the 'laws' not only of their own genetic inheritance but of evolution, in a way that we are not. Such an assertion sets buzzing a whole hive of questions. It may be that the world would be a better place, and would have a much more secure future, if this disturbingly innovative species *homo sapiens* had never appeared in it. The fact remains that we do have this faculty, and it can be used in a host of different ways. These divide into two naturally opposed groups. It can be employed creatively; it can also be used for self-indulgence. We are all familiar with the idea of the creative imagination, though we tend to distance ourselves from it. Its opposite, fantasy, is also familiar to us, more familiar than we often recognize. Each of these concepts will have to be examined more closely.

It may seem at this point that all I am doing is making an arbitrary distinction to satisfy, or impose on others, my own criteria of what is good or bad: the right and wrong uses of imagination. What after all is wrong with fantasy? At worst a harmless form of relaxation, at best it is a stimulating and enlivening source of entertainment. If, as most people will say, we cannot all be creative, why should we be denied the lesser pleasures of the imagination? But there is more at stake than this. Not all self-indulgence is to be condemned; and the creative imagination can be put to some pretty appalling ends. The real issue is not a moral one. It can, I believe, be demonstrated that there is a real connection between one use of this faculty and one peculiarly, distinctively human characteristic of our species, which is our freedom; and that the

8

converse is also true, that there is another and very different use of it that can lead to a reduction or even, eventually, a total loss of that freedom.

Before looking further into that issue, however, I want to deal with what may for some people be a real difficulty: the idea of the creative imagination. This is commonly seen as the distinctive preserve of genius; of the artist, the poet, men and women of special gifts whom we may honour (especially when they are dead) but can hardly presume to treat as our equals. This is a sad mistake.[3] Each one of us is born with a potential for imagination, a potential which, as with our other gifts, intellectual or physical, will naturally vary from one individual to another, and will in any case depend for its full development on education and other social forces. Nevertheless, the germ of it is there from the start, that capacity for conceiving that the world, and our life in it, need not always be the way it is now. Most of us when we consider Mozart or Rembrandt, or even such figures of our own time as Solzhenitsyn, Michael Tippett or Henry Moore, are conscious of an enormous gulf separating us from them. Yet what we have in common with them is much greater than we generally realize. It is not just that the experiences they celebrate are, basically, the elemental stuff of life the world over. If this were not so, we should never respond to them the way we do. The joys and sorrows that they articulate, though with more intensity and precision than we could ever hope to do, are still the joys and sorrows of our everyday life; they do not belong to some higher sphere of intellectual or aesthetic sensibility. All this is true; but there is more. The very activity of creation which we surround with such a mystique should be recognized as evidence of our common humanity. It is, or could be, part of the daily experience of each and every one of us.

Think for a moment about what happens when you sit down to write a letter, especially one in which you try to express some depth of personal feeling. By the time you have

9

got to the bottom of page one you will almost certainly have put into words things that you had no clear idea of when you started. In the act of writing something has begun to take shape – something out of which something else now begins to emerge. But is this what we mean when we talk of the creative imagination? Before we allow ourselves to be persuaded that there is some perfectly 'natural' explanation for all this – the unconscious, for example, is a great standby for those who like to regard such mysteries as 'purely psychological' – we should reflect that even in this simple, everyday situation we have brought something into being – the letter – which was not there before. True, it can be demonstrated that we often have knowledge that we are unaware of having which can by certain techniques be brought to the surface of consciousness; but it is a considerable step to go from there on to believe that all creative thought can be explained without remainder in these terms.

Here is another example. Consider what may happen in a simple conversation between two people.[4] Of course it often happens that each just wants to put across his or her own point of view. But it can be quite different when both are genuinely concerned to let the truth take shape out of the encounter. When this is so, the starting point of each, the motive if you like, becomes lost sight of in the excitement of a common discovery. Thoughts and insights emerge which neither of the participants could have reached on their own. Here again some psychological explanation may seem plausible, but we must not be fooled into believing that such an interpretation can wholly account for the fact that in each of these examples there has been what might be called a $2 + 2 = 5$ situation. That letter cannot simply be explained in terms of the intention of the writer plus the materials used for its writing. Even more clearly in the case of the conversation, the sum of the parts – the individual contributions of each participant – is not enough to account for the resulting whole; and as we know from experience the equation may feel much more like $2 + 2 = 7$, or

12, or 17. That creative bonus remains a mystery beyond explanation or prediction.

Experiences like this may seem too trivial to be described in terms of the creative imagination. What have they in common with *The Brothers Karamazov* or the Mass in B Minor? That link has still to be demonstrated. The point is not that each of us may be a little Bach or a potential Dostoevsky but that what we share with such great men is a capacity for discovering more about ourselves and the world, and for giving expression to those discoveries, that cannot easily be accounted for. Those who still cannot bring themselves to believe in their own creative imagination are selling themselves short. The Gospel parable of the talents was not told for the benefit of those who have five talents or those who have two, but for those who have only one and see no potential in it. In fact our religious tradition is rich in reminders of the significance of the insignificant: the still small voice, the one coin lost, the grain of mustard seed, the single sparrow that falls to the ground. So perhaps we should learn to give more value to these experiences of an unaccountable remainder, and to that faculty in ourselves that can bring it to our attention and enable us to explore its possible significance.

It still remains to be seen how this imagination can relate us to the mystery. It may be creative, but how can we tell that what it creates has anything to do with reality, with that ocean that touches our lives at every point? Or is that too just 'pure imagination', a comforting or nostalgic illusion spun like a cobweb out of our own daydreams? Questions like these cannot, as I have said, be answered by proof. But it may be that where demonstration falls short conviction may take over: the kind of conviction that comes home to one from what we may call telling experience. Experience can only tell us anything, however, if we are prepared to take it seriously: seriously enough to call into question some of those common-sense habits of thought which tell us not to be silly; of course things like that do not happen, whatever can we be thinking of? The creative imagination in fact is the open imagination, the imagination that prompts us to think the unthinkable, to conceive the inconceivable, to imagine the imaginable. It is thus our natural, inborn faculty for transcendence, for rising above the limits of what previously seemed possible.

This is what might be called the vertical imagination, the faculty that enables us to raise our vision to new heights or to explore more deeply the roots or bedrock of our being. But experience will also tell us that this same creative imagination is no less important to us as an essential means of communication, as the faculty by which these vertical insights may be, so to speak, extended laterally, may be shared, may be made available to our fellow men and women. So a language, or rather languages, of mystery come into being, by which the individual can have his or her personal sense of mystery confirmed by the discovery that others too have had some experience of it themselves.

Experience can also tell us of the shipwreck that the individual, or even whole societies, can come to if the imagination tries to break wholly free from the influence of tradition. To believe that you can rediscover the universe from scratch is no less futile than to believe that you can do without a shared symbolic order (verbal or otherwise) of communication. No less disastrous, though, and more prevalent today is the belief that a tradition can survive and be kept alive without continuous exposure to the creative energies of the imagination. That interaction is liable to be disturbing; it is also itself something of a mystery. It is a mystery, however, in which we can all share.

But that participation will involve work, and it is with the nature of this work, and the reasons we too often find for opting out of it, that some of the more difficult sections of this book will attempt to deal. At least they have been difficult to write. If they are difficult to read, the fault may be mine. On the other hand I should myself be very suspicious of any writer who offered easy answers to these questions. It is, after all, the nature of mysteries that, unlike problems, they do not have solutions.

So the language of mystery turns out to be something of a mystery itself. That does not mean, however, that we should not do all we can to clarify our thinking about it. Far too much that is written about spirituality virtually concedes that precision is not possible in speaking about this area of human experience. The dominant prestige of science has deceived us into thinking that it is only quantitative analysis that can achieve true precision. It can certainly convey that impression, but generally only by selecting from the phenomena under observation those aspects which are amenable to such analysis and ignoring the rest. In fact, so far from having a sharp cutting edge, quantification can be a pretty blunt instrument unless it is preceded by acuteness of observation. Consider this:

Something slobbered, curtly, close,
Smudging the silence: a rat
Slimed out of the water and
My throat sickened so quickly that

I turned down the path in a cold sweat.
But God, another was nimbling
Up the far bank, tracing its wet
Arcs on the stones.[5]

Could any observation be more precise than that? Seamus Heaney has a true poet's eye for detail. Look at those verbs: 'slobbered . . . smudging . . . slimed . . . nimbling'. And if it is objected that this precision is aesthetic rather than scientific, what does that tell us about science? That it has no need for this kind of sensitivity?

My object in quoting this is not to pick a quarrel with science. Scientists have enough problems of their own. What I am anxious to counter is the view, not generally of course made explicit, that a certain reverential obscurity is appropriate to any discussion of the spiritual life. That view is too often encouraged by the tendency, already mentioned, of those who have had any profound spiritual experience to say that it is beyond words, a statement which their own words regularly show to be untrue.

There is also another point. To confuse the language of mystery with the mystery which that language is attempting to probe and articulate would be to abandon any claim to objectivity. Not that objectivity is in itself always the most fertile of ideals, but the alternative is to concede that there is no reality in this mystery beyond the subjective imaginings of the minds that seek to apprehend it. That would be simply not true to the explicitly expressed convictions of countless individuals who have declared their experience of the mystery to be the most real thing that had ever happened to them.

* 2 *

Imagination and Fantasy

I have never liked or even understood the fantastic or romantic elements in themselves, nor have I believed in their existence as an independent domain. . . . For me art is a possession, and the artist is a man stricken, possessed by reality.

Boris Pasternak[1]

It was Coleridge who first, in England at least, spoke up for imagination as having an essential part to play in our perception and understanding of reality, with his well-known distinction between the primary and the secondary imagination, and then again between imagination and fancy.[2] But his thinking on this, as indeed on many other subjects, was not as lucid and systematic as it might have been. So let me start with something nearer to our own expeience.

We are all familiar with the idea of 'motive'. Motives are what move us. We never do anything without any motive at all. Often of course our motives are mixed, more mixed than we realize, and one of the great achievements of psychology has been to show us how powerful an unconscious motive may be. Some will go further than this. If we are to believe the behaviourists, everything that we do, without exception, can be explained in terms of some antecedent motive or determining influence; so that nothing in our behaviour is without its cause, of which that behaviour is the predictable effect. At least it would be predictable, if we had a complete knowledge of all the causes. This is very plausible. A lot of the time it is true. I am thirsty (cause), so I go to the pub (effect). I have academic ambitions (cause), so I accept an invitation to read a paper to some learned society (effect).

All the same we all have a feeling deep down that we cannot so easily be explained; that we do have some freedom of choice. This conviction remains even when we recognize the various motives that are continually at work in us. The more we are aware of them the better equipped we are to cope with them, or choose between them. Or so it seems. But can we go a stage further and conceive of any action that is entirely free from this motivational web? I have said that we never do anything without any motive at all. Can we ever reach a level at which we can truly say that our only motive is to be free from all motives? Rarely, perhaps, in this absolute sense; but it is not so rare, I suggest, for this kind of freedom to be a significant, and sometimes a controlling, element in quite everyday activities.

What I am saying is that there are some human actions that are not done for some pre-existing cause but in order to bring something non-existent into being. We may still, if you insist, speak of motives, but in this case they are motives that draw us on from in front, rather than driving us from behind. Here though I think we should drop the word 'motives' altogether, because the essence of this kind of action is that we cannot clearly identify what the cause of it is because at the time of the action that cause does not yet exist. The effect, that is, actually precedes the cause: its purpose is to bring that cause into being.

Is this mysterious? Perhaps; but as I have already shown (in the writing of that letter, the creative exchange in that conversation) it is a mystery that we can all find to be part of our own daily experience. In each of these cases, and in many more once we begin to notice them, <u>we can recognize this ability of ours to open ourselves up to new and unsuspected possibilities; possibilities that we have the power to turn into realities.</u> In doing this we are able to get free, in some degree at least, from those causes which drive us on from behind, and to let ourselves be guided by some freely chosen end, though precisely what that end is is still hidden from us.

It is important at this point to be clear that the distinction being made here is not the classic one between efficient and final causes. A final cause, or purpose, may seem to lie in the future; but when I am asked, 'What are you doing that for?' I can generally give an answer which shows that I know what I am aiming at. My intention, that is, can be specified from the start; it already exists before the activity which is designed to bring it about. Such an intention may well be an expression of my freedom; such a freely-chosen intention may be contrasted with those drives to which we react unthinkingly, instinctual forces which we share with other animals. That distinction is no doubt important. There is no reason to believe that other animals are capable of the kind of reflection that enables them consciously to formulate a purpose and then to seek the means of achieving it. It may even be that we are strictly speaking wrong in attributing intelligence or even thought to other animals. The question here is not where we draw the line between human consciousness and that of other animals. That can wait. My immediate point is to show that our freedom can be limited not only by those 'lower' motives we share with animals but also by our supposedly 'higher' powers of reasoned thought. Both efficient and final causes, that is, can constitute motives. In each case, the cause precedes the effect. What I am trying, with some difficulty, to identify and describe here is that capacity we have for reversing the process, for launching ourselves into an action without having a clear and distinct idea of what precisely the end will be. It is the ability to remain in this state of suspended expectation, and to maintain it through long periods of concentrated activity, that is characteristic of all truly creative achievement.[3]

play

All this can throw useful light on the difference between fantasy and the creative use of the imagination. As this is a difference on which I shall be putting a good deal of weight, let me straight away admit that it is one that is almost impossible to state with any precision. For a start, any attempt to define imagination as a specific mental faculty, on a par, say, with reason or intuition, is doomed from the start. Like a tot of whisky poured into a glass of water, imagination, for good or ill, pervades the whole of our lives. It can be used creatively, and so help the growth of our freedom; it can also be subordinated to motives of every kind, and so serve to undermine that freedom. If I use 'fantasy' for the latter, that use of imagination that serves our more easily identifiable motives, and keep 'imagination' for that creative activity that is open to the unknown, the still-to-be-discovered, I realize that I shall be using a shorthand that may not only be confusing, because of that mixture of motives from which we can rarely ever escape, but is also quite arbitrary, since in common speech we do not make such a clear distinction. It may even be offensive, if it suggests that fantasy is bad and imagination good. Each in fact has potential for both good and evil. Fantasy of course can take many forms, some of which are at worst quite harmless and may be extremely enjoyable; life would be the poorer without them. If I seem here to be somewhat severe in my judgments it is only because the good can often be the enemy of the best. If we are to recognize the imagination as the highest of all gifts, that by which alone we can attain to any new perception of reality, then we cannot permanently be satisfied with any lower employment of it.

Let me start with fantasy in its crudest form. I lie in my bath, relaxed and luxuriating in the warmth, and I start picturing to myself what I should like to do to old P. who behaved so intolerably to me yesterday; what I shall say to him when I next meet him, how humiliated he would be if he knew what other people really think of him, and so forth. A scene forms, perhaps a whole sequence, that is very gratifying to my ego. My fantasy is the product of all the desires, fears and frustrations by which, consciously or unconsciously, I am motivated. I am constantly driven by them. In real life I cannot let them have their head, but now, in the privacy and security of my bath, I can let them loose. I may even think of this as therapeutic; I may feel it does me the world of good to let my feelings take over for the time being. Here at least I need set no bounds to my self-indulgence; here at least I am completely free.

Nothing of course could be further from the truth. My freedom has been abandoned to those compelling motives that my feelings about old P. have spawned; so far from being free, I am entirely in their grip. And as for my self-indulgence having no bounds, it is pathetically limited; I am now less able than ever to get away from this tight little circle of resentment and vindictiveness. This is the danger we run when we abandon ourselves to fantasy: we remain ego-bound. It changes nothing; we are the same people after as before – even more so, if that is not too absurd a way of putting it. We may for a moment feel better for having given way to our feelings; afterwards we shall probably be all the more resentful, when our little trip is over, to find the real world, and even worse the people in it, as tiresome and intractable as ever.

Fantasy does not always take such petty forms. In the respectable guise of poetry and art, especially in the Romantic tradition, it can even aspire to a certain nobility. You remember FitzGerald:

Ah Love! could thou and I with Fate conspire
To grasp this sorry Scheme of Things entire,
    Would we not shatter it to bits and then
Remould it nearer to the Heart's Desire![4]

This is the perpetually recurring dream of humanity: if only, if only. . . . But the idealist's vision may be as futile as anyone else's fantasy if that 'Heart's Desire' turns out to be just one more mix of those all too human passions that drive us on from behind. Why else is it that political revolutions that set out to champion the cause of freedom so often end up by establishing authoritarian regimes that are no less repressive than those they have overthrown? In contrast to this, the true idealists in politics are often derided because they cannot specify exactly what they hope to bring about.

It is of course only addiction to fantasy that is in the long run dangerous.[5] Most of the time we do not take our fantasies that seriously: we dilute them with the cold water of common sense, so that like a good sundowner they help us to relax pleasurably after a hard day's work; they can take the edge off the stresses of life. But they can also take the edge off our imagination. I can use a chisel as a screw-driver (the very thought makes a sculptor wince); I can also employ it to pare my nails or sharpen my pencils – uses for which it was never meant but not immediately ruinous. But why use this most powerful and delicate of instruments on things that have no need of such fine steel? Science fiction is a case in point. The vast bulk of it aims at nothing higher than entertainment; its immense sales testify to its success. The more wildly imaginative it seems to be, with its time-warps and simultaneous universes, offering us escape from the laws of physics and any other tiresome limitations that cramp our little twenty-four-hour days, the more successful it is in distancing us from reality. Not just the reality of the 'real' world of commuter trains and income tax demands, but from any other. For thousands it provides an acceptable substitute for any genuine exploration of the world of the spirit. It can so easily be read as implying that, once free of the restraints of the physical universe, anything goes; if nothing is impossible, nothing too fantastic to be true, then no fantasy is more true than any other fantasy. Who ever thought it was, anyway?

I realize that I am being grossly unfair to a small handful of writers such as Stanislas Lem, Ian Watson or Ursula Le Guin who have used the language and forms of fantasy in genuinely creative ways, not to give us a holiday from the human condition but to prompt us to probe it more deeply, to reveal in it something of that infinite potential that being truly human holds for us. Fantasy of course being only one use of this faculty of imagination cannot easily be isolated from any other when that imagination is working at full bent. The kind of writers I have mentioned stand in an honourable line that runs through Charles Williams and H. G. Wells to Spenser and Dante, indeed right back to Homer himself. The worlds they create may seem fantastic, but they do not ultimately, in Pasternak's words, 'believe in their existence as an independent domain': independent, that is, in the sense of existing without relation to any human situation. They use the language of fantasy not to encourage us to escape from ourselves but in the end to send us back to reflect more deeply on what we have it in us to become as human beings. If the freedom that fantasy, pursued for its own sake, offers us is a delusion, what the truly creative imagination can do is to set us free, to open us up, or more precisely to enable us to open ourselves up, to an infinite world of possibilities:[6] to reality. So when Pasternak speaks of art as 'a possession', and the artist as one who is 'stricken, possessed by reality', what undoubtedly he has in mind is this capacity in us all to be taken over by reality, to be released, if only for a moment, from the ego-bound world by which we are most of the time possessed. It is thus not only the artist and the poet who are capable of this freedom; we are all able, being endowed with this faculty of imagination, to some extent to create, and continually to recreate, the world in which we live.[7]

This same faculty of imagination can be seen at work at every level of human life. It may be called for in all sorts of everyday problems. This tin-opener that has got caught up inside the washing-machine (the things some people keep in their pockets!); how on earth am I going to get it out? This demands the practical imagination we call ingenuity. There is another kind we call curiosity. Why has the liquid in this test-tube gone cloudy? It should have stayed clear. Throw it away and start the experiment again, the unimaginative chemist will say. Wait a minute, says the more imaginative one; something has occurred to me. Things occur only to the receptive mind. 'Occur': a word with an interesting history. It is the Latin *occurro*, I run to meet. Do we take credit for things that occur to us? Or do we feel that there is somewhere some kind of initiative, running to meet us?

This is not just a language game; because in their wider, deeper search for a meaning behind phenomena, for a pattern, perhaps even a purpose, in that total openness of mind that can put off if only for a moment all preconceptions, men and women throughout history have sensed that the universe is not a closed system; it has come home to them that reality is ultimately something more than a mindless interaction of random forces, as in some great inner city wasteland in which survival is the best we can hope for, and 'the life of man solitary, poor, nasty, brutish and short'.[8] Thomas Hobbes is generally admired as a great political realist, and it might seem impertinent to question this, still less to suggest that he lived in an unreal world of fantasy. Yet in the last resort he did fall short in imagination, that spiritual openness by which men and women of far lesser intellectual power than he have become aware of a reality that comes to meet them, of a mysterious initiative that responds to, perhaps even anticipates, their search. They may even speak, if they are philosophers, of a First Cause, an Unmoved Mover, and that not in the Deist sense of some Great Artificer who wound up the clock of the universe and left it to run, but rather as a continually available source of power, and apparently love, beyond space and time yet 'closer than breathing, nearer than hands or feet'. 'I hear voices telling me what to do,' says St

Joan in Shaw's play; 'they come from God.' 'They come from
your imagination,' replies Robert de Baudricourt. 'Of
course,' Joan says; 'that is how the messages of God come to
us.'⁹ (Shaw's own judgment comes in the epilogue to the play:
'Must then a Christ perish in torment in every age to save
those who have no imagination?')

It may be objected at this point that this elevation of
imagination itself into a mystery (as distinct from the mystery
it may open us up to) can only obscure our understanding of
what is a perfectly normal and intelligible element in our
human make-up; one, moreover, that needs to be looked at
with all the clarity we can, since in all probability it is here that
the dividing line between man and other animals is to be
found: in this development of consciousness to the point at
which the mind can reflect on its own experience, learn from
it, and change it. There is in fact much in the operation of the
imagination which can be clarified by careful observation and
analysis – which is what I am here attempting. But if the
imagination is a mountain whose lower slopes offer pleasant
pasture and easy cultivation its peaks are covered by perpetual
snows. It may even, like Mount Olympus, have its head
hidden in the clouds. The analogy claims too much if it
suggests that the upper heights of the imagination are the
natural abode of the gods. Nevertheless I believe we shall sell
the imagination, and ourselves, short if we stop our exploration at the snow line. To conceive of the imagination simply as
the power to form images or concepts is not enough. To the
painter Kasimir Malevich the highest function of the artist was
to create 'forms of perfection' – an effort that always ended in
frustration, since in the act of creating such a form the artist
comes to recognize that perfection cannot be contained in any
form. So it is the peculiar gift of the imagination, and its prime
function, not to keep its eyes on the horizon but to speculate
continually on what lies beyond it; not simply, as the word
might suggest, to create images, or even to pass from one
image on to another, but to conceive of a reality that may be

beyond all conceivable images. If this is a paradox, it is no more than we should come to expect in the spiritual life, at the level which any statement we may make about ultimate reality needs, apparently, to be complemented by its opposite: the paradox succinctly put by St Nicholas of Cusa when he declared that 'it is beyond the coincidence of contradictories that Thou mayest be seen, and nowhere this side thereof'. [10]

I spoke just now of a 'spiritual openness'. [11] The word 'spirituality' is used today in a variety of ways. In the present context it seems legitimate and useful to keep it to indicate that particular characteristic of our species that, apparently, distinguishes us from all others. Just as we find sexuality in many life forms, but not in the amoeba, there is something that we seem to find in human beings and in no other living creature. So we may describe ourselves as spiritual beings, as being capable of spirituality, by virtue of this capacity to be open to a dimension of mystery: [12] a mystery, what is more, that seems for some inexplicable reason to have given us, each one of us, some tiny element of its own essential nature, its own spirituality.

To speak of the mystery in such personal terms may be to anticipate a conclusion that some will feel to be premature. Nevertheless it is a characteristic quality in the experience of those who live by the imagination that what occurs when things go right is felt to be some kind of gift, whether in the laboratory or in the studio or in the everyday encounter of two human beings. (The theological term for this gift is of course 'grace'.) The most complete form this awareness can take is to be seen in those rare individuals for whom the whole of life is experienced as such a gift. You may remember how, at the end of Georges Bernanos' story *The Diary of a Country Priest*, the young man lies dying, and another priest is sent for to give him the last sacrament, ordained by the church as the formal means of grace. But he cannot be found. 'Qu'est-ce-que cela fait?' says the dying man; what does it matter? 'Tout est grace'; everything is grace; everything is a gift.

At this point it may be said that what I am here describing as imagination in its highest form is more properly to be called faith. For instance it could be said that imagination can take us thus far, to the limits of the imaginable, and that it then must give way to faith which enables us to go forward into the unknown, the unimaginable. It would of course be absurd to reject a concept so central to our whole tradition, and it may be that there are many who will find this way of speaking more appropriate to their experience. There are however two reasons why I have not so far found it necessary to introduce the ideas of faith.

First there is the danger that to give too high a value to faith may devalue imagination. We may even be urged not to put our faith in imagination but in something higher. The accusation of Pelagianism, the heresy that we can attain to God by our own human efforts alone, without grace, is clearly implied. But if imagination is conceived of as that very openness to grace, then to put our trust in it is no more and no less than to have faith in what may be revealed to us through it. This little semantic problem could perhaps be solved by saying that imagination is the essential means, humanly speaking, by which faith becomes possible.

The second difficulty is more serious. In common speech faith often implies an element of belief. So we talk of 'the Christian faith', suggesting a more or less explicit structure of beliefs, the acceptance of which will distinguish a Christian from, say, a Muslim. In the same way we speak of 'other faiths'. These credal differences may remind us that faith can also be seen to operate at a cognitive level, and this gives the psychologist the opportunity to identify different stages of faith through which the developing human being may pass on his or her way to maturity.

This concept of faith then is both rich and many-layered, but also potentially ambiguous. It should certainly not be seen as a rival or alternative to imagination. My concern is to bring into clearer focus the part the creative imagination has to play in the growth of that total commitment to which the word faith tries to do justice.

It is all very well, though, to speak about a total openness as the proper state of the receptive imagination, but as every religious tradition has recognized there are forces operating at the spiritual level that are neither benign nor creative. Popular Christianity in our time has rather lost this sense; but in Hinduism Shiva the god of creation always has by his side his destructive consort Kali. Wordsworth could speak blandly of 'a wise passiveness'; in our own century we have surely had too many reminders of the negative, not to say demonic, forces that may be at work not far below the surface of human consciousness. There is no knowing what turns the human imagination may take if left on its own. We cannot simply identify spirituality with the imagination; we cannot take it for granted that the imagination will by itself know to choose the good and to refuse the evil. As a philosopher might put it, imagination is necessary to the development of spirituality, but it is not sufficient. It needs support.

The danger about speaking of particular human faculties is that it suggests a mechanical model of the mind; as though it were composed of separate interacting parts, as the carburettor, cylinders, battery, fuel pump and so on go to make up the internal combustion engine. This habit can perhaps be traced back to Plato, with his tripartite scheme of reason, spirit and appetite; but neither he, nor certainly his mentor Socrates, ever lost sight of the fundamental unity of the human mind (or psyche as they would have put it, though that word again has in modern times acquired overtones that they would not have understood). To be safe, we should use adverbs in preference to nouns; we should speak of people thinking imaginatively or rationally, emotionally or intuitively, rather than distinguish these activities in terms of particular faculties, let alone areas or hemispheres of the brain. That said, I propose to go on using these convenient abstractions, on the understanding that they are not taken too literally.

So when I say that the imagination needs the support of, say, the reason, what is really meant is that for any balanced or comprehensive understanding of life we should not rely uncritically on this open receptivity which is the distinctive feature of the imagination. Clearly we need as far as possible to act in every situation as whole human beings. That is easily enough said. What it implies, though, is more complex than may at first appear. It means more than just 'getting one's act together', becoming personally integrated, individuated or whatever the current jargon may prescribe. The support that the creative imagination requires is social as much as internal.

Earlier on I made a distinction between the 'vertical' activity of the imagination and the 'lateral': terms that, again, should not be taken too literally and do not attempt to do more than indicate the multi-dimensional life of the mind. Few of us in fact lead perfectly balanced lives, and in terms of introversion and extroversion the needs of every individual will be uniquely different. Nevertheless we can all probably think of examples of people in whom a rich and active inner life finds no equivalent expression in relation to their fellow men and women. There are doubtless many more than we realize. Alienation, however defined, is only a pathological form of what is a common, almost a distinguishing feature of many modern societies: a spiritual loneliness.

It is ironical that in a culture that has developed the technology of communication to an unprecedented degree this sense of individual isolation should be so prevalent. There are some, of course, who are not worried by it. Loneliness only afflicts those who have not learnt to be alone. Generally speaking, though, it is hard for the individual to go on believing in his or her own spiritual experience without the assurance that something like it has happened to others. How otherwise can one be sure that it really happened, that it was what it seemed to be at the time? There are all sorts of reasons that can make it harder for one to keep faith with the insights of that private inner world. When Sir Alister Hardy, the

founder of the Religious Experience Research Unit (now the
Alister Hardy Research Centre) died, some of the most
moving tributes to him came from those who expressed this
sense of deliverance from isolation. Now at last they could talk
about their experience.

> I feel sure that many like me who experienced 'astonish-
> ment of heart' will thank you, above all, for releasing us
> from the feeling of being alone and isolated. Now we know
> that there are thousands like us in this country alone,
> probably millions, keeping quiet but sharing, and occasion-
> ally discovering each other. I am aware of a boundless
> gratitude to Sir Alister. I often think about it and the way he
> released me to enjoy what might have been a bewildering
> burden.

> I can still remember my astonishment when I first heard of
> the project, and I began immediately to regard in a new light
> those hidden things stored away in the dark recesses about
> which I never uttered. How many of us he must have helped
> 'to come in from the cold'![13]

Why could they not talk freely about it before? Part at least of
the reason was, and still to a great degree remains, the lack of a
language, an acceptable way of sharing and communicating,
whether in word, symbol or ritual. It is one thing to discover
that such experience is common to humanity. That in itself can
be reassuring. More important than this, though, is to find
ways in which the energy locked up in that experience can be
given creative expression: creative in the sense we have already
noted, when a result emerges which is out of all proportion to
what each has put into it. None of this can easily happen
outside the supporting structure of a living tradition.

* 3 *

Tradition and the Work of Art

The words 'tradition', and even more, 'traditional', are apt to arouse strong feelings. They are commonly associated with concepts such as loyalty, or its opposite, betrayal. They may also be highly divisive: the 'traditionalist' is one who stands by what he has learnt to value from the past, and has no truck, it is implied, with those who threaten it with innovation of one kind or another. These are extreme attitudes, but it is too often characteristic of those who uphold tradition to see any kind of compromise as something to be resisted.

All this is very sad. No human society can prosper without tradition, but tradition if it is to be kept in good heart needs constantly to be rescued from those who would preserve it from change. Just as we are the only animals that can imagine a future different from the present, so we are the only ones that can learn from the past. There are of course other species that do learn to adapt their behaviour to changing conditions, but none appear to have our ability to reflect on our own history, and to learn from it. At the political level this is not always very evident, but we have learnt to grow sweeter apples, and to make sharper chisels, not to mention lasers and computers. Another name for this learning from the past is tradition. Without tradition, the handing down of acquired skills and wisdom, we should be less than human, just as we should be without imagination.

These two, imagination and tradition, are in fact intimately dependent one upon the other. Just as the imagination, left to itself, may follow fruitless paths, so tradition, which is a distilled essence of the imaginative discoveries of the past, needs, if it is to stay alive, to be continually revitalized from the same source. This is evident enough in our technological development; tragically our spiritual tradition has not, in recent centuries at least, shown the same openness to creative renewal.[1] All too often, within what once could be called Christendom, those who have felt themselves most immediately responsible for the well-being of their tradition have seen their duty largely in terms of conservation, not just of a 'truth once delivered to the Saints' but also of the language and symbols and ritual forms, not to mention the social organization and physical structures of their churches. It is becoming increasingly common for churchmen to speak of 'the Christian heritage'.

It is most misleading to think of a tradition simply in this way. An inheritance is what the dead have chosen to leave the living: the living have no choice in what they receive. A tradition, on the other hand, is what the living think to be worth preserving from the work of the dead: a very different matter. Nobody today reads the complete works of Isaac Newton. His voluminous expositions of theology, let alone his incursions into alchemy and astrology, are of little interest nowadays except to the student of the eccentricities of genius. What we have taken, and preserved, of Newton are his physics and his mathematics, though even these are not now regarded with the same veneration as they once were. In this continual process of selection from the past much is continually being shed. Inevitably errors of judgment are made. (Some are irretrievable, like the loss of so many of the tragedies of Aeschylus.) That is why we need museums and archives, to see that nothing is permanently lost, to be a resource that future generations may go back to. But nobody wants to live in a museum. It is only a living tradition, not an embalmed one, that can give the creative imagination the support it needs. And that support is mutual.

It is mutual because it is only by the constant injection of new imaginative insights that a tradition is kept alive. Unless the seed fall into the ground and die. . . A spiritual tradition that is not ready to see all its outward structures destroyed, all its conventional forms of expression abandoned, to give room for the growth of the new is already moribund. This may seem a harsh demand. Are all the magnificent achievements of the Middle Ages and Renaissance to be scrapped, and replaced by modern equivalents? Of course not. It is the readiness that matters. What has to be replaced is the spirit of antiquarianism that is simply not open to the possibility that the language of the contemporary imagination may carry a revelation for the twentieth century that the language of earlier centuries does not. Mary Richards goes to the heart of the matter:

> In spirit, the artist (by whom I mean man in his creating aspect) like the saint (by whom I mean man in his adoring aspect) gives away all he has: possessions and human ties – in order to be open before Presence. Or, if you prefer, in order to be constructive. This act is, in its own way, destructive of worldly forms. I see forms constantly perishing in the perpetuation of life. This is the spirit of regeneration. It works within us constantly. Let us cooperate with it, finding in it the fulfillment of our love. It is a sacrifice. It is a sacrament, celebrating the mystery of matter.[2]

The dilemma is perhaps more acute for the Christian than for any other religious tradition because of its claims to a once-and-for-all historical revelation. Yet those who speak about 'the Christian revelation' as though it left no more to be said have not begun to see the problem.[3] It is all very well to quote those texts which warn us of truths that are hidden from the learned and shown only to the humble, to be understood only by those who become as little children. The Gospels themselves, those springs to which all Christians must keep returning for the refreshing of their faith, contain paradoxes which are not always faced. Here is an example: belief in the resurrection has led naturally to belief in Christ as a permanently available presence. Did he not assure his followers that he would be with them till the end of the world? Yet no less explicit was his insistence to his friends, not long before his crucifixion, that he had to leave them, and that this would be for their own good; otherwise the Holy Spirit would not come to them, the Spirit that would guide them into all truth. Can it be that an over-literal adherence to the historical Jesus has left the church less open to the renewing spirit?

In fact the name of Jesus Christ is probably uttered today by more millions of humanity than ever before, but not all of those who use it regard him as the source of any revelation. The air around us is all the time vibrating with a great variety of radio or television waves to which the unaided ear is quite insensitive. Unless we have a receiver that will enable us to tune in to one channel or another we shall never be aware of their existence. So with the revelations of the Spirit. The French philosopher Gabriel Marcel in a beautiful image spoke of the infinite possibilities of grace 'scattered like pollen on the summer air'. But there can be no fertilization until that pollen reaches the flower that is ready and able to receive it. There can be no revelation until the message of the Gospel reaches those who have ears to hear it and eyes to see it. And it is not going to do this until it is given living expression, and that not once and for all but continually anew in each generation. Last year's pollen is no use.

It should in fact be more natural for Christianity than for any other religious tradition to have a positive relationship with the arts, particularly those which, like painting or sculpture, pottery or weaving, draw directly on the material world for their means of expression. A conviction of the basic goodness of the creation is built into the whole Judaic tradition: God looked upon his work and saw it to be good. For a Christian, belief in the incarnation of the divine in the human figure of Christ reflects also an acceptance of the rest of creation as in some way embodying that same creative energy. One of the major concerns of the early church was to combat the view, represented by Manichaeism, that spirit alone was good and matter either indifferent or evil. That battle has never been permanently won, and at a time like the present when verbal forms of expression and communication are so predominant in our religion, the need, and oppor tunity, for the physical embodiment of faith has never been greater.

For all his Puritanism Milton was no despiser of the senses (it was he who first introduced the word 'sensuous' to the English language); and when he went blind he wrote of 'wisdom at one entrance quite shut out'.[4] If the idea of sensuality is ever to be redeemed from its by now habitual association with sin (and one particular kind of sin at that) the arts may be the only means we have of rediscovering the wisdom of the body, to balance and enrich the wisdom of the mind.[5]

Up to now in discussing the creative imagination I have emphasized the part it plays, or can play, in the lives of us all, as a faculty we all in some degree share. All the same, in every society there are those whose exceptional gifts, whether in art or music or literature, seem to set them apart from the rest of us. That distance may not always be as great as we think; nevertheless these individuals do have a special part to play in the renewal that a spiritual tradition requires if it is to be kept alive. To say that tradition and imagination are interdependent, that the one depends for its health on the other, may make neat sense in theory; in practice the opposite often looks more true. When the word is taken in its usual sense the 'traditional' is by its very nature resistant to imaginative invention. It is only in retrospect that we can see the great innovators like Berlioz or Wagner, Constable or Cezanne as being deeply in debt to their tradition; to their contemporaries they seemed more often to be subverters of it.[6] For us today it is much easier to see how they helped to transform it. So, if we are going to understand tradition as a living force we must somehow get free from this reactionary model and see how it can nourish rather than stifle the imagination. It is easy enough, as I have said, to see growth at work in the technological field; market forces make sure of that. What concerns us here is what the conditions are that make for the free growth of a language of mystery.

In what follows I shall start with the visual arts. Though they raise problems of their own this is because they illustrate in a particularly acute form the inertia and spiritual entropy that afflicts so much of our life today.

It is the function of the original artist, says John Berger, to renew the tradition to which he belongs.[7] The passion for originality has spread like a notifiable disease among those who work in the visual arts today, chiefly because, unlike poets, say, or composers, they produce works that can be collected as investments. This has brought into being a market of dealers and galleries and auction houses who depend for their very existence upon the regular production of new material – new in the sense of being immediately distinguishable from all that has gone before. 'Ah, that's a Schnabel you've got there, I see.' Ridiculous, but also tragic; because the search for originality belongs to the realm of fantasy, that ego-driven world in which the desire to make one's mark in the world outweighs any vision of an end still to be realized. It is that vision that the genuinely imaginative artist or poet will serve, often at the sacrifice of his or her reputation in the market, and so will make it available, in a language (verbal or visual or musical) that is accessible to the men and women of his or her time. Accessible, but not without some effort. This is not an argument for socialist realism, that one style of art that all totalitarian regimes employ to sugar the pill of propaganda, or for reducing all music to the level of pop. So far from reducing his or her language to make it intelligible to the insensitive, the original artist may well make even greater demands on our attention simply by having something new to say or to show to us. We are all likely to be resistant to innovation. But where the need to communicate is stronger than the desire to be original, the genuinely creative artist or writer will ransack all the resources of his or her tradition in the search for some means, any means, of expressing an insight that conventional forms will no longer do for. The end result of that search will be a work of art.

All this may only reinforce our original suspicions that the world of the artistic élite is not for us. Before long someone will start talking about aesthetic values. Here once again we must resist the temptation to deny our own creative responsibilities. True, the language of art-talk has often been elaborated by philosophers and professional critics (the latter not always innocent of that commercial obsession with originality) to an esoteric refinement that borders on the ridiculous. So let us start with this one common, basic phrase, 'the work of art'.

It is in fact a marvellously rich one, compact with unsuspected meaning. We are familiar enough with its common use to describe those objects – paintings, drawings, carvings and so on – to be found, for reasons not immediately obvious, in museums or art-galleries. (Take them out of that context and their standing may well be less clear.) But what about the arts of literature or music? We may know where to find the Mona Lisa; it makes no sense to ask where Shakespeare's Macbeth or Bartok's Sixth Quartet are to be found. This should immediately make us question our easy assumptions about the visual arts. Plays and music depend for their continued existence, in one sense at least, upon performance, which is a kind of re-creation of the original. Performances are often described as faithful, which implies some degree of commitment in the performers. They may even be called creative or even revelatory, which suggests that there are depths in the original text still to be discovered by a more insightful interpretation. (It is interesting to note that many composers have been notably ineffectual performers or conductors of their own works: Schubert and Schumann are well-known examples.) When Walter Pater said that all art aspires towards the condition of music, he could have been foretelling the rediscovery in this century of abstract art. This movement has, like many others, produced a great deal of triviality, but at its best it recalls us to face one central truth about all true art, which is the demand that it makes on our own imagination. The work of art is not one that is over and done with when it leaves the artist's studio. That is where our work has to start.

So it should come as no surprise to find artists often speaking of their finished work as not an end but a beginning. Here is what the sculptor Naum Gabo says:

> A work of art, restricted to what the artist has put into it, is only part of itself. It only attains full stature with what people and time make of it.[8]

Bridget Riley is even more explicit:

> Someone who practises as an artist makes a work but he does not make a work of art. This is done by others: a two-way act is needed. A sort of alchemy turns matter into spirit, and the arena for this transformation is provided by exposure. Unless the work is 'seen' in the fullest sense of the word it is obliged to remain a physical object, a personal document or perhaps an idiosyncratic preoccupation. Nobody can truthfully claim to possess a work of art because in

essence it belongs to all. Nor can the community at large claim it, because each work has to find for itself those who respond to it, those who see it, and those who belong to it.[9]

The artist who perhaps felt more passionately about this than any other was Mark Rothko. He was convinced that his paintings depended for their very life on the attitudes of those who owned them.[10] In the hands of someone who did not respond to it, or who treated it simply as a financial investment, a picture would actually, he felt, be diminished, its very life drained out of it; whereas in the home of an appreciative owner it would continue to grow, infused with new life and vitality. (When he died there were over seven hundred unsold paintings in his studio.)

The work of art, then, is not something done once and for all by the artist or the poet. True, we may need them to start it; but they also need us to continue it. If a tradition is really to be renewed, a special responsibility lies upon the original artist, the original poet, the original composer, to take the initiative; but there is a similar responsibility upon the rest of us to recognize and respond to that initiative. But what do they originate? What they set moving, if that tradition is in good health, is a far-reaching movement whose end they cannot possibly imagine, because its continuation does not depend upon them. Yet essential as is the role of these singularly gifted individuals, they differ from the rest of us only in degree; otherwise there would be no possibility of communication, no possibility of that 'two-way act'. They may sometimes seem to breathe a more rarefied air, but the world they inhabit is the same world as ours. We can make their discoveries our own. We can, to use Kierkegaard's word, 'appropriate' them.

To appropriate something means to take it for your own use, to make it your own. It is just the right word for this aspect of the work of art. There is something very personal about it; it also suggests something not quite straightforward, something slightly underhand. When I buy a railway ticket I do not then appropriate it. So the work of art is not done at the level of some public transaction – that level at which it would be quite wrong for me to appropriate your ticket. The common laws of property do not apply to the work of creative communication. In the legal sense, yes: the writer has the copyright of his own work (though he may delegate it to his publisher), the painter has some control over the reproduction of his pictures. But the real work goes on in an altogether different dimension, one in which such rights do not apply. Quite the opposite in fact. There is a generosity about true works of art. They give to us all that we wish to take, all that we feel we can use, free and for nothing.

But no, not really for nothing. Both the giving and the taking are costly in terms of effort. Just as the artist has invested not just time and labour but his or her whole self in the work, so must we who approach that work, if we are to have any hope of taking anything worthwhile from it. There must be an equal investment of attention – and creative imagination – on our part. The work of art may begin with the artist: only the individual who is capable of penetrating most profoundly into his or her own experience and extracting, distilling from it some essential concentrate is able to touch others at that same level. It will only continue if they in their turn are ready to do the same work on themselves. We know a poet, said Coleridge, because he makes us poets.[11] What the poet does, that is, is to activate in us our own capacity for what the Greeks called POIESIS, making. If I am ready to meet the poet on his or her level, I shall find a resonance being set off in myself. Something will be stirred in me, even though the actual thoughts, feelings or insights that come to me will probably be quite different from those in the mind of the original maker. This is because the dimension in which all this occurs, this 'alchemy that turns matter into spirit', to use Bridget Riley's words, is the dimension of human freedom. Released by my own imaginative openness into this new dimension I am set free to discover more of myself; to explore that same ocean which touches us all, but particularly to discover in it what is of special significance to me as a person, so that I may myself set out on new voyages of discovery on my own.

Nothing in fact is more rewarding to any artist or poet than to have someone quite unknown come up and say what his or her work 'really' means. That meaning almost always comes to the artist as a complete surprise, and the more surprising the more exhilarating; the more powerfully does such a response confirm him or her in the conviction that something worthwhile has been achieved; that true POIESIS has taken place. A boost to the ego, yes, of course, but also an immense strengthening of that belief, often so desperately needed, in the validity of the imagination and its power to reveal a world to whose reality others will now bear their own independent witness. Thus the American sculptor Anne Truitt writes of 'that passion for learning how to make true for others what I felt to be true for myself'. And she adds: 'I cannot remember, except very, very early on, ever not having had this passion.'[12]

So there is this interdependence between the artist and the rest of us. It is not just financial support that artists need to keep going; they can be starved in other, less tangible ways.[13] (Financial security can even be the ruin of an artist when it is offered by a commercial gallery which lays down its own conditions: a regular supply of marketable produce.) A more seductive illusion of support is given by the veneration of a cultured élite. There is no questioning the near-religious respect with which a relatively small section of our society today regards the work of the 'great' artist. Such works, whether in museums and art galleries, those 'churches' of modern art, or more especially when acquired as personal possessions, may become the object of a contemplation which, though solitary, fulfils many of the functions of a religious ritual. The artist is then given the role of prophet; indeed he or she may consciously assume that part. I call this support illusory; at the time, of course for the individual who is the focus of it, this attention may be highly gratifying, besides being financially rewarding. However the history of art shows how few individuals who have been accorded this status have continued to produce work of any significance. The élitism which this worship of art engenders is not in the long run healthy for either the art or the religion of the society in which it develops.[14] Not only is it divisive; it is liable to inhibit that free interchange of imaginative energies that characterizes a genuinely creative community. Most cultures can look back to some golden age of artistic or literary achievement. In fifth century Athens it did not just happen that so many exceptionally talented men emerged in a single generation: it was the creative involvement of a whole society, or at least a large section of it, that made possible that extraordinary flowering of genius.[15] In Germany after the first world war a similar ideal inspired a group of artists and craftsmen to set up the Bauhaus. But its base was too narrow, and it was not securely rooted in a living tradition. 'We still lack the ultimate power,' wrote one of its leading members, Paul Klee, 'for the people are not with us. But we seek a people. We began there with a community to which each of us gave what he had. More we cannot do.'[16]

'Each gave what he had.' This is how a tradition is kept alive. Some people talk as though tradition were some kind of inert deposit, accumulating over the years by a natural process, like sedimentary limestone. But there is nothing automatic about the growth of a tradition; if it is to be kept in good health it must be by a continuous process of organic renewal.[17] A living human body only maintains life by a regular replacement of old cells by new. When it is no longer capable of this it dies. Most people live in happy ignorance of this. For years, centuries in fact, the view of the body as a self-regulating system, like a complex machine that only needs attention when something goes wrong, has dominated Western medical theory and practice. Only recently have we begun to see body, mind and spirit as a whole, and to understand ourselves as having a responsibility for our own health. This does not mean dispensing with doctors. Nor should we be ungrateful to those who love their tradition and try to prevent its dissolution. But too possessive a care for its preservation can, as we know, lead its self-appointed guardians to cut off these very energies by which it can be revitalized. It is too late, no doubt, to rescue the word 'traditional' from the traditionalists; but is there any other word available that will bring out this dynamic element in tradition that alone will keep it alive? Those who are interested in the history of words may care to reflect that tradition and treason come from the same root. Each in its now different way means a handing over. To be ready to let go of a tradition may in the end be the only way of showing faith in the spirit that can renew it.

* 4 *

Art and its Enemies

how should contented fools of fact envision
the mystery of freedom?

e. e. cummings[1]

Learning the language of mystery, then, involves a particular
kind of work: a work that is itself a response to someone else's
work. A response, not a reaction. Reactions are more or less
conditioned or determined by the stimulus that provokes
them; they are predictable. A response is essentially a human
act. Of course a great many of what we may think of as our
responses are little more than reactions; our freedom to
respond is limited by that web of motivations from which we
never wholly escape. But if the creative imagination is that
faculty by which we can open ourselves up to possibilities still
unrealized, the faculty by which we can reverse that mechan-
ism of cause and effect and so get away from that gravita-

tional pull of all that lies behind us, then participation in the work of art is one of the most valuable exercises we can possibly undertake if we want to develop our full humanity, to discover the potential of our own freedom.

I have already tried to show, in distinguishing between imagination and fantasy, how illusory the freedom is that the latter promises. A very similar deception can be practised by much of what often passes as art. It is in fact a very good test of the claims of any such work, whether visual or verbal or in any other medium of expression, to ask how far it really appeals to our freedom; how truly it invites a response rather than a reaction. It is not, I think, too much to say that there are certain quite identifiable enemies of art. The more clearly we learn to recognize them the better we shall understand the need to keep the language of mystery unaffected by them.

The first and commonest of these enemies of art is imitation. It may not be the most insidious, but it is certainly the most popular. 'What exactly is that picture of?' The question assumes that the purpose of a work of art is to convey some information, to be a more or less accurate description of a particular scene or object, to record the actual appearance (whatever that means) of a person or an event. The same with poetry: 'What exactly is this man trying to say?' As if the difficulty of the poem were the result of the writer's failure to communicate his or her experience accurately, to correspond with our own. But 'art does not reproduce the visible; it makes things visible'. So Paul Klee. Its purpose, and justification, is to open our eyes to aspects of the world, or ourselves, that we have not yet noticed, not to mirror back to us what we already know. Georges Braque makes the same point: 'L'art est fait pour troubler; la science rassure.'[2] In a world where science is far from reassuring many people will turn to art for a confirmation of their own familiar view of life; for comfort, not for trouble. Beauty, the creation of which has classically been regarded as the purpose of art, is too often defined in terms of what produces these feelings of comfort; of what

43

relaxes tension, not of what creates it. The result is an enervated spirituality; the cause is an art reduced to imitation.

Imitation, sometimes called naturalism or realism (though the last term begs the question: what reality?), was the degrading ideal of much British painting of the last century. Pictures like Millais' famous 'Christ in the Home of his Parents', better known as 'The Carpenter's Shop', attempt a truthfulness to detail that leaves nothing to the imagination. A perfect 'visual aid' to a scripture lesson, it has no doubt done years of service in Sunday schools. There is only one possible interpretation of its imagery: we are free to do nothing but accept what Millais tells us. In fact the 'realism' is laughably unreal: the figures are so delightfully English, and the whole scene recalls a 'tableau' in a village pageant. Perhaps for this very reason the picture is still widely regarded with affection. Thousands of well-brought-up Christians have been imprinted with its message, that that is how it must have been.

The same imitative ideal can inspire literature – as in those Victorian novels in which every detail of the heroine's beauty is painstakingly recorded – or even music. It is also powerful in the cinema. At first sight the camera seems capable of nothing more than automatic realism; hence the long resistance in Art colleges and elsewhere to the acceptance of photography as a form of art. In fact from its very beginning it proved as capable as any other medium of that art of illusion that can offer one meaning on the surface and quite another to those who will stay to see beyond it.

Another enemy of art is rhetoric. The widespread if still often grudging acceptance of 'modern art' has by now persuaded enough people to question the imitative ideal, so that it perhaps no longer merits the place of enemy number one. Rhetoric, however, pervades our whole visual environment. Sometimes it is blatant and unashamed, as in advertising or political propaganda; sometimes it is quite unsuspected, and this is when it is most insidious. Rhetoric is of course the technique of persuading other people that what you say is true, or worthwhile, or admirable. In the television commercial, whose exploitation of the medium is often so much more arresting than the old films it interrupts, it persuades us that we have needs we never thought we had. In the party political broadcast it persuades us that we understand the issues and can trust those who have made them clear to us. It also appears in religion; the reason why so few sermons ever reach the level of art is that the preacher is generally more concerned to put across his or her own point of view than to help us form one of our own.

In all these forms it is not hard to see the threat that rhetoric poses to our freedom. Those who pride themselves on being aware of it – those crude appeals to our greed, vanity or prejudice – are by no means immune to it. We may all be more vulnerable at an unconscious than a conscious level. There are times when to be believed is less important than to be remembered. Besides the obvious one already mentioned its uses in religion are many and various, and they are as old as history. Mediaeval frescoes that illustrate the torments of the damned and the rewards of the faithful served precisely the same purpose as the emotive eloquence of the twentieth-century evangelist does today. Religion has always exploited to the full the media of its time. As General Booth asked, why should the Devil have all the best tunes? A well-known modern firm of religious posters has been notably adroit in adapting the visual techniques of the commercial, with all their sentimentality and more, to pious ends.

And why not? The trouble is that the immediate impact of rhetoric has continually to be reinforced or it is liable to wear off. You can't fool all the people all the time. Hence the continual pressure that authoritarian regimes have to maintain to preserve the 'purity' of their art, their music, their literature. Freedom, like a weed in a well-kept garden, is native to humanity, and will most naturally express itself in imaginative forms that do not accord with the gardener's plans. There are echoes of this in our religious situation today.

In the hands of a true artist the didactic tradition of church art could once be combined with a new and enlarging vision. It requires a great effort and much specialized knowledge to realize what a shock such painters as Giotto or Masaccio gave to their contemporaries. It was by such shocks ('L'art est fait pour troubler') that the tradition was given new life. Soon little was left except the didacticism, and a great mountain range of religious art declined rapidly to what it is today: the flat level of a visual aid.

As can be seen in Socialist Realism, the one manner of art approved by all dictatorships, imitation and rhetoric are natural allies. Neither encourage the imagination to stray beyond authorized limits.[3] There is however another and quite different style in which rhetoric plays an equally dominant part. This is expressionism.[4]

All '-isms' must be mistrusted. When named after a man (Marxism, Freudianism) they generally represent a fairly limited segment of their hero's views. When based on an abstract concept (romanticism, mysticism) they too often assume a precision in the original idea which is simply not there (what is a romantic? a mystic?), and offer a whole philosophy constructed on that unsound foundation. Expression in one form or another, define it as you like, is present in all art. Even Malevich's painting of a white square on a white canvas expresses something. The danger of making the expression of feeling (another dangerously imprecise word) the dominant function of art (or poetry or music) is that the feeling expressed, or more usually the emotion, being regarded as an end in itself, can easily be assimilated by others without requiring any of that work of art by which it can be appropriated in a creative way. The powerful emotional involvement often to be witnessed at great political, sporting or even some religious occasions may well not touch its participants at a level deeper than that of fantasy: that level at which our feelings are still determined by pre-existing motives. In one of his less happy excursions outside the field of theology Paul Tillich saw in the contemporary expressionist school of painting a new hope for twentieth-century religious art.[5] He even went so far as to declare Picasso's *Guernica* to be 'a great religious picture'. It is in fact a highly rhetorical work to which, whatever its other qualities, it is difficult to respond, or should I say react, with any other emotion than that which gripped the artist at the time it was painted, and that was a feeling of violent anger.

A third enemy of art is journalism. The journalist writes for today. Yesterday's story is cold; tomorrow's – well, tomorrow is another day. When the values of journalism encroach on art, questions of fashion, taste, relevance and of course originality begin to take over. These are all distractions from that work on which our spiritual growth depends. Fashion reflects what is socially acceptable; it is all to do with conformity, nothing with self-discovery. Taste, well, no artist of any worth ever gave a damn for good taste, which like fashion is really only concerned with what is or is not done, or said, or worn.[6] Relevance has rather more claim on our attention, but it is astonishing how totally irrelevant most of the art and literature of the past now seems which set out to stir the nation's conscience or catch the tide of public feeling. Dickens survives in spite of the crusading humanitarianism which first made him famous.

Yet there is a paradox here, well stated by Regamey: 'A work or art is timeless only if it truly belongs to its own time.'[7] Like those canaries that coal-miners used to take down the pits to warn them of poisonous gases (the canaries, being more sensitive, would die first) the true artist or poet can have a prophetic role. There are times when this takes over, absorbing all the creative energy. But we do not think of Jeremiah as a journalist, nor think the worse of Wilfred Owen for writing in the preface to his poems: 'All a poet can do today is warn.' Less often quoted is the sentence that follows: 'That is why the true poets must be truthful.' But the truth he offers does not only lie on the surface. True, there are times when his writing makes its chief impact at this level. But we do not value his work only, or even principally, for its vivid evocation of the horrors of war. Rhetoric and journalism combine with devastating effect in 'Dulce et Decorum Est':

> If you could hear, at every jolt, the blood
> Come gargling from the froth-corrupted lungs,
> Obscene as cancer, bitter as the cud
> Of vile, incurable sores on innocent tongues –

but this assault on our feelings is not poetry; it leaves us no option but revulsion, no freedom to reflect on anything but the picture he thrusts under our noses, from which he is determined we shall not escape. Contrast with this the true poetry of his 'Insensibility', in which Owen has distilled from an experience no less deeply felt an 'emotion recollected in tranquillity'. To this we are free to respond in circumstances far beyond the context of its original composition. Its relevance is universal. No one can escape the realism of 'Dulce et Decorum Est', but here in contrast is a truth that we can all appropriate in our own ways.

> But cursed are dullards whom no cannon stuns,
> That they should be as stones;
> Wretched are they, and mean
> With paucity that never was simplicity.
> By choice they made themselves immune
> To pity and whatever mourns in man
> Before the last seas and the hapless stars;
> Whatever mourns when many leave these shores;
> Whatever shares
> The eternal reciprocity of tears.[8]

To speak of imitation, rhetoric and journalism as enemies of art may seem over-dramatic. It may even be misleading if it suggests that the creative imagination should have nothing to do with such vulgar activities. But there is something, in the largest sense, vulgar about the work of the creative spirit. It is liable to cock a snook in the most embarrassing way at our established standards of propriety, and even of truth and morality. What I have chosen for attack are three particular pathologies in each of which a perfectly healthy and even necessary function is allowed to get out of hand.[9] Pretty obvious targets, most of them. It is not difficult to show how our freedom can be infringed by these abuses of the imagination.[10] It is much harder, in fact it is quite impossible, to demonstrate how it can be enlarged by participation in the work of art. This is, as I have said, because in the dimension of human freedom nothing is predictable, neither what will happen nor whether anything will happen at all.

Whether anything will happen will depend on the openness of the individual imagination; what will happen will depend on the unique qualities of each personality, in relation (or out of relation) to his or her fellow human beings, each one of whom, if their imaginations are even a little bit open, will be as unpredictable as the next. In practice, of course, we are all socialized to share some degree of common understanding not just of words like 'orange' or 'bicycle' (where the degree is high) but also of 'paucity' and 'simplicity' (where it is a good deal lower). Otherwise there could be no communication at all. But these words are just the bricks, which have to be reasonably uniform if any building is to be possible. When we come to ' . . . whatever mourns in man Before the last seas and the hapless stars. . . . Whatever shares The eternal reciprocity of tears', to agree on what the individual words mean may get us some way, but all it can do is help to define a space, a space that is up to us to fill, or not.

In contrast to this, the work of your typical expressionist is likely to be so full of the painter's own feeling that there is no room for yours.[11] No room; no space. This space is what true art in its generosity provides, without laying down how we are to use it or what we are to fill it with. Of course we can still fill it with our private fantasies, as when we 'identify' with a character in a Mills and Boon romance. We may of course do the same with *Anna Karenina*. The difference is that Tolstoy's characters are so spaciously and generously drawn that we cannot identify with them without finding ourselves having to live up to them. They are larger than life as we have up to now experienced it. It is then up to us to fill the space that Tolstoy has created.

If a great master of realism can achieve this, so also can abstraction in art create such space. All art, even the most naturalistic, is to some degree abstract. Even in our everyday perception we regularly ignore most of what we see, paying attention only to what we are looking at, and even then we disregard many qualities in the object that do not interest us. So every percept is to some extent a construct. The artist takes the same process a step or many steps further, stripping away whatever may interfere with the particular vision of the world that he or she wants to present. This stripping away is abstraction.[12] Carried to extremes it may seem to leave nothing that recalls the familiar visible world. But even the purest geometrical abstraction contains elements that relate to our experience, if not of nature then to the man-made world that for many today is the more familiar background to their lives. A common criticism of so-called abstract art is that 'you can read anything into it'. But this is just what the artist hopes for; that space is for you to fill. It may happen, especially with some minimalist art, that the painter or sculptor does not provide us with enough to get that 'two-way act' started.[13] Nor do titles like 'Composition No. 6, 1978' help to get a meaningful dialogue going. But just as a profitable investment policy may mean taking risks, not all of which come off, so here; we may invest our attention in works that in the end do not repay it. But to take no such risks means to cut ourselves off from one important source of creative renewal; and anyway the effort will not have been wasted. We all need to keep the muscles of our imagination in good shape.

This distrust of abstraction is in fact curious in a society that has for centuries lived among some of the finest works of abstract art ever created. Nobody complains that the great masterpieces of Gothic architecture lack feeling. Perhaps this is because these are places where it is already assumed that people go to work: the work of prayer and worship. I would not want to suggest that that work is the same as the work of art. Nevertheless they have much in common; if you are good at one you may well be good at the other. Architecture does indeed create space; it also, at its best, creates imaginative space, so that the physical sense one may have of being in a well-designed building, whatever its actual size, can lead to a freeing of the spirit, an awareness of new possibilities, an enlarging of life. We shall return to this theme in Chapter 7.

* 5 *

Symbol, Sign and Sacrament

It must begin by now to seem that one aspect of this subject has had quite enough attention, if not too much. Must the language of mystery always involve so much work? Is freedom always to be so hard won? If human beings are by nature spiritual creatures, why need the language of spirituality be so complicated?

One answer to this could be that it is only the description of this language that is complicated, not the language itself. There is some truth in this. A circle after all is quite difficult to describe or to define; yet, to look at it, it is simplicity itself. This comparison, though, could be misleading. It is the profound simplicity that lies at the heart of all spiritual experience that could be said to be represented by that circle. A recurring element recorded by many people who have felt frustrated at being unable to describe their experience is a sense of loss, or exclusion. This is particularly strong in relation to childhood experience. This feeling is not to be dismissed as mere nostalgia. Or if it is nostalgia, that longing may be not so much for the simple joys of those early, less complicated days as for a far profounder simplicity to which the imagination of childhood may be open in a way that becomes progressively more difficult as the years pass. I shall return later to this 'nostalgie de Paradis'. The point here is that even at the best of times men and women have groped for words in their struggle to express the heart of an experience which still somehow seems to elude them. And these are not the best of times.

Physicists, since Kepler, have used the word 'inertia' to mean (and here I quote the OED) 'that property of matter by virtue of which it continues in its existing state, whether of rest or uniform motion in a straight line, unless that state is altered by external force'. There are those who seem to believe, as we saw in Chapter 3, that a spiritual tradition will, if protected from alteration by external force, continue in its existing state. The consequence of that belief is inertia of a very different kind, inertia as the layman commonly understands it: inactivity. It is the complacency that is pretty well satisfied with the way things are. These are indeed not the best of times. We have too long been treating the spiritual language of the past as a heritage to be enjoyed, living on capital without concern for its depreciation. So we must not complain if there is work to be done. There always was; today there is more than ever.

A common symptom of this complacency is the way some people talk about symbols. Yes, they will say, we know that ordinary language will not do for these mysteries; that is why we need symbols, to help out when the words and concepts of everyday speech fail us; symbolism is the language of mystery. So far so good; the trouble is that symbolism is too often seen as something that can be used, as the solution to a problem. What might be called the instrumental view of symbols takes no account of the potential energy concentrated in them, and of the creative commitment required of us if that energy is to be released into life; it makes no distinction between symbols and signs.

Here again, as before with fantasy and imagination, these two words are commonly used without regard to the distinction that needs to be made. My analysis may seem arbitrary, but, however we finally agree to use those words, what is important is to understand the two very different degrees of engagement that may be involved.

A symbol is in some ways like a metaphor: it stands for something other than itself. A metaphor can illuminate what it stands for, as when Yeats speaks of 'the fury and the mire of human veins'. It may take some time to see what he is talking about; when we do, we learn something new about ourselves. But metaphors can die, and then pass unnoticed into the common stock of everyday language. (That sentence contains at least two dead metaphors.) So can symbols; they then degenerate into signs. They can still communicate information, but they will have lost their power to open new doors in the mind.

A symbol, however, is more than a metaphor.[1] Metaphors operate at the level of simile; they suggest a likeness you had not thought of before. A symbol has a greater power of concentration: a single word or image, object or action can act as a focus for a variety of possible meanings or associations. While a metaphor 'stands' for something else, a symbol does that and more. It can have a kind of magnetism to attract ideas; like a magnet it can be charged with energy. We have no language sufficiently dynamic to describe this properly. We may call something symbolic; we may say that it symbolizes this or that. But we have no word to suggest the process by which that power is given to it. We do not say it is 'symbolized' as we say that iron is magnetized. The creation of symbols is a mystery, like the origin of works of art. What concerns us here is not so much how they come into being (convention has an important part to play in that, as we shall see) as how their life can be maintained and the energies they hold be drawn upon, and also renewed.

First, however, there is another question. How is a symbol different from a sign?

Most signs are specifically designed to give clear and un-ambiguous information. The word 'Gentlemen' put up in a public place should leave no doubt as to what it indicates. So also with non-verbal signs, though many people would call these symbols, like the ⇌ now familiar to us outside railway stations. Signs can be found in the natural world too, as when heavy clouds foretell rain, or changes in the behaviour of animals indicate the onset of the mating season. A good sign has only one meaning. A good symbol, on the other hand, may have many possible meanings. A symbol that can only mean one thing is not fulfilling the function of a symbol, which is as I have said to be the focus of a whole cluster of meanings, all related in some way to one another, but varying with the different interpretations of different people. This is because what a true, living symbol appeals to is, like the work of art, our freedom. The life of symbols is always precarious; they can so easily sink to the level at which they have just one meaning, and become signs. They may then still be useful as a means of conveying information; they will no longer make any positive contribution to the language of mystery.

Another indication that a symbol is moribund is when it is used as decoration. How often do we see the cross, once the central and most powerful symbol of the Christian tradition, used for purely decorative purposes. There are hardly any items of church equipment – pews, hassocks, books, furnishings, vestments, architecture – that may not at some time be adorned with it. Sometimes it is repeated to form a pattern, with very elegant effect. A well-known modern English cathedral has a very finely designed cross on the outer wall of its eastern end. Perhaps the space would have looked too bare without it. And of course it serves to show that this building is a church. But really, its only function there is decorative. This kind of thing is now so common as no longer to seem remarkable. What harm can come from this use of symbols as decoration? The answer should be obvious. If symbols are really to be part of that language by which we explore and express the mystery of creation, then any practice that tends to weaken or degrade them is a most serious matter. When a symbol is employed as no more than a unit of decoration, what is potentially a thing of power is reduced to being a means of pleasure. That is the purpose of all decoration, as it is of all entertainment. Life would be the poorer without either, but let us not fool ourselves. Neither decoration nor entertainment point beyond themselves; all they do is allow the eye, the mind, to rest agreeably in the present. As entertainment fills time that we have nothing better to do with, so decoration fills space that might otherwise disturb us by its vacancy. Used for this purpose, symbols that might have been able to confront us with mysterious or disturbing realities become defused, their power dissipated and lost.

At least we describe it so; in fact it is we who become immune to their impact. But this state is not, in theory, incurable. Most of these symbols are man-made. We might call them conventional, if that word were not associated with all that is lifeless, artificial and lacking in any spontaneous feeling. Convention implies agreement. Perhaps we have agreed too easily, or too long, about what these symbols represent. Perhaps now we can agree on the need to break through that hard crust of habit and expose ourselves to the energies of which they may still be the channel. This too calls for work: work not unlike the work of art in that the creative imagination will need to be in good order. Symbols however are not generally created by individuals. They are more often the expression of dogma.

Dogma today has a very bad name. This it does not wholly deserve. In the early church it meant acceptance, or consensus. When dispute arose over some article of faith the issue would be hammered out until some statement acceptable to everyone was reached. This was, in Greek, *dedogmenon*, what seemed right. There was no question of coercion. If some people then persisted in disagreement, something had to be done about it if the unity of the church was to survive. Pressure had to be brought to bear. It is what was done then, and later, that earned the word dogma its evil reputation. To be dogmatic today means, ironically, to have abandoned the original spirit of dogma. There can of course be no communication of any kind without dogma, in its original sense: some degree of consensus on language, taking that word in its broadest sense. If the language of mystery is essentially a language of imagination, it is no less essentially a language of, in its most practical sense, love. By enabling those who share it to express what they have in common it will enrich and keep warm their sense of community. So it will need to be a language (visual, musical, ritual as well as, perhaps even more than, verbal) basic enough for everyone in the community to understand and use it. This need for simplicity will always make for tensions between those who wish to see that language reduced to the level of the humblest understanding and those who feel it their duty to maintain its full charge of meaning. This is why symbols are so important; with their many-layered potential of interpretation, they can bring the learned and the unlearned together in the expression of a common purpose.

All this puts a tremendous weight on the symbolic forms and actions that are to represent the core of religious belief and practice. Few questions in the history of the Christian church have caused such heart-searching, and been so divisive, as the meaning of the sacraments. The teaching, for example, that in the mass (eucharist or holy communion) the element of bread and wine become, or represent, the body and blood of Christ has at times been regarded as so central to the life of the church that the most strenuous efforts have been made by different denominations to establish its 'true' interpretation, and to bar from participation in the sacrament those who do not subscribe to that interpretation. Yet how is meaning to be found in this doctrine if the imagination is to play no part? There is clearly a danger, if too strict a conformity is insisted on, that the material elements in the sacrament will be reduced to the level of signs, to have a specific and limited meaning beyond which the mind is not encouraged to inquire.

There are no easy solutions to these questions. They illustrate vividly the relationship, and the tensions, between the freedom of the imagination and the discipline of tradition discussed earlier on. From the outside, from the objective point of view of the legislator, this will call for compromise and self-denial. Seen from the inside by those personally involved, the situation will seem more like a creative dialogue. Concern to preserve the purity of sacramental doctrine can lead to the kind of extreme conservatism already noted: the desire among church leaders not to risk anything that might water down or distort the truth that for them and generations before them has been mediated through the sacraments. This in its turn can lead to a ghetto mentality in the religious community, when the survival of a faithful remnant in face of the pressures of the world comes to be seen as an achievement in itself. In such an atmosphere symbols are likely to be treasured with a devotion never far from nostalgia: a sign that what Nicholas Berdyaev called the 'great falsehood of static'[2] is beginning to harden, and may end up by choking, the arteries of the spiritual life.

Survival, though, may seem no bad thing to those who have no creative vision of the alternative. Anyway, it will be said every society has its periods of quiescence as well as of growth. As tides come in and go out there will be times of dryness when life must somehow hang on until the flood returns. So through the Dark Ages religion in Britain is supposed to have survived by withdrawing to the monasteries. Perhaps in our time too it should be content to hold on and wait for better times. Not so. No one should take comfort from this kind of talk. For one thing, it is bad history. The so-called Dark Ages in Britain are now known to have been a time of remarkable creative achievement, even though the church that inspired it had sometimes to withdraw from the rest of society. And what signs are there of such creative energies at work among Christians today?

The truth is that what movement there is seems largely to be in the opposite direction. Here is a frank comment from two recent American writers:

> The towering fact about art and Christianity today is that they have got along without each other for about two hundred and fifty years now and neither appears noticeably the worse for the absence of the other. . . Art is not really necessary to Christian salvation at all. The Church can get along without art. [3]

Not everyone is as explicit as this, but are not Frank and Dorothy Getlein saying what the great majority of church men and women believe today? A generation or so ago it was the latest thing among theologians to maintain that the truth of the gospel could only be discovered in its pure form by a stripping away of the poetic and imaginative forms in which it had originally been expressed. Demythologization was the word: get behind the myth to the reality. This way of thinking may now be on the decline in academic circles. Perhaps it never got far beyond them. Yet a very similar trend seems to lie behind some of the liturgical reforms of the last few decades. The desire to put everything into familiar, no-nonsense language is a clear indication of a movement away from the rich complexity of symbolism towards a supposedly easier but certainly a more impoverished form of communication.

These are in fact only the most recent phenomena in a process that set in long ago. Two hundred and fifty years is a modest estimate. What is surprising is that after all this time we still have no word in English to describe one of its most typical, most widespread and most insidious aspects: the growth of kitsch.

* 6 *

Kitsch in Art and Ritual

When a language adopts a word of foreign origin[1] it is presumably because the object or idea it denotes is also felt to be alien. Something is no doubt to be learnt about Anglo-Saxon attitudes to eating when we note that the words for many dishes, and even the places where they may be eaten (restaurant, café), are taken from French. So what about the cheap, sentimental art so prevalent in our religion, for which we have imported the German word 'kitsch'? It may indeed be possible to trace some of the most sugary Christmas-card imagery back to popular German religious art of the early nineteenth century. Perhaps it started to come over with the Prince Consort and the Christmas tree. At any rate, the stuff has been well-established in our own church life for many years. That it has flourished here for so long without a name suggests that our religious tradition found nothing uncongenial in this particular kind of sentimentality. Its assimilation appears to have passed unnoticed. This does not mean that we have become immune to it. On the contrary, we have been taking it into our systems like some toxic radiation for years without suspecting any harm. Only now have we begun (if indeed we yet have) to recognize the debilitating effect it may have on our spirituality.

But are the results really so serious? These things, it will be said, are only the outer wrappings of the faith: I mean those mass-produced figures of the holy family, of angels and shepherds, in plaster or plastic; those pseudo-mediaeval stained glass windows full of lifeless, sexless humanity; those pietistic hymns with their guilt-laden texts, banal melodies and sickly harmonies. To lump all these things together may be unfair. Some are doubtless on the way out, though many religious bookshops, especially at centres of pilgrimage, show how little popular taste has changed over the years. New techniques of photography and film have widened the scope of modern kitsch; its spirit all too often remains the same.

What right, though, has anyone to take up a superior attitude? Does this really do all that amount of harm? Quite the reverse, it may be claimed. Such things as these have for years helped countless simple people to say their prayers; they have gone to make up an environment without which, for many, worship is not possible. For others, again, they are associated with deeply affectionate memories of childhood, of family life, of long years of church-going; with the formation in fact of a whole way of life which we ought to be the last to despise. So what right have we to lay down standards or criticize the judgment of people who are happy to express their religious faith in these forms we find so deplorable? Are we not, once more, failing to observe those biblical warnings about the truths hidden from the wise ones of this world and revealed to the foolish? Aesthetic judgment is surely one thing and spiritual understanding quite another.

The last thing to be encouraged is the kind of patronizing arrogance that will allow anyone to plead the low standard of the music or the architecture as an excuse for not going to church. Nor would one want to see some standard of good taste laid down, to be defined no doubt by the appropriate committee, to which religious art or literature should conform. The only religion that will worry about good taste is one that has become reduced to a social institution, one that has allowed a concern for the likes and dislikes of its members to take priority over its concern for the mystery – a mystery that utterly transcends any regulations we may devise for its expression but which can be known by those whose spirituality has been opened up in response to the work of the creative imagination.

This is the crux of the matter. Art is a means, art is the means, of telling the truth. Bad art does not just fail to tell the truth; it substitutes a lie. When Christ is portrayed as a characterless figure of sentimental benevolence surrounded by cuddly lambs in a romantic landscape, what effect does such a representation have on the prayers, let alone the theology, of those for whom he is a focus for worship? Kitsch degrades by satisfying the heart or mind with an inadequate or false image of reality.[2] It is this, and not its failure to appeal to the finer feelings of a cultivated mind, that makes it an enemy of true spirituality.

Kitsch can be simply defined as sentimental art;[3] but then, how is sentimentality itself to be defined? It is an easy defence against any direct appeal to our emotions to call it sentimental. But why do we agree that *Home Sweet Home* is sentimental but not, say, the Beatles' *Eleanor Rigby*? Or Benjamin Leader's notorious *February Fill-dyke* but not Constable's *Flatford Mill*? Are these simply matters of taste that will vary from one period, or person, to another? Obviously the expression of feeling that one individual or society will find tolerable may be intolerable to another. To say that the feeling expressed by sentimental art or literature is false will not by itself be enough. Even the image of 'gentle Jesus meek and mild' can claim some historical authority. Sentimentality is more accurately to be defined as partiality; its fault is that it does not tell the whole truth, but only that part of it that we want to see.

This understanding of sentimentality reveals its close affinity to cynicism, which again is the attitude of those who cannot bear to look at life in its wholeness. Sentimentality and cynicism are in fact two sides of the same coin: the one is blind to the evil in the world, the other to the good. If sentimentality was the prevailing weakness of much Victorian art and literature, that of our century has been dominated by a cynicism that gives respectability to many now well-known names. So Mendelssohn, say, and Picasso may have more in common than they seem to: each man supremely gifted to show his contemporaries that side of reality they wanted to see, that side to which they were partial.

It may have been noted that I have had very little to say on the subject of beauty, an omission which would have been unthinkable in any such study as this a century ago. Nor do I now propose to offer the kind of definition that will appeal to philosophers. But as a guide to where true judgment lies in the middle ground between sentimentality and cynicism one could do worse than consider Kathleen Raine's statement: 'Beauty is the real aspect of things when seen aright and with the eyes of love.'[4] This emphasis on reality implies a wholeness of vision in which desire may have a place but can never dominate, desire being essentially a form of partiality.

The double meaning of this word partiality can remind us of the affinity between sentimentality and fantasy. We are partial to what we have already experienced ('I know what I like'), so the past determines the present; we are not open to the future. But past experience can never be more than partial; it is only through the open imagination that we can glimpse the whole.

Most of this has been said before, but even when shown up for what it is the appeal of kitsch is unlikely to be much affected. This is not just because there is something of the sentimentalist or the cynic in all of us – we cannot see life steadily and see it whole all the time – but because kitsch is itself only a particular example of a more widespread infection that will always threaten a tradition in decline. It is always easy to point to the superficial charm of kitsch, its cheap sensation-alism, its gift-wrapped commercialism. All these are easy targets. They are also the wrong ones. If it is to be eradicated we must expose not the sentimental kind of naturalism it delights in but the dangers of naturalism itself.

We have already seen what may happen when art is dominated by an imitative ideal. The consequences are bad enough at any level of imaginative expression. In religion they are liable to be particularly damaging. The dangers of a naturalistic art have been recognized in more than one religious tradition. Both Judaism and Islam from the start banned any visual representations of the deity. Why must God not be so represented? Because he cannot; because an image is a likeness, and God is beyond any possible likenesses. He is what he is; he will be what he will be. In Christianity too there have from time to time been reactions, sometimes violent, against the use of images in worship, though a religion that puts so strong an emphasis on incarnation is always going to have ambivalent views on iconography. However if the ultimate object of worship is conceived of as beyond any literal representation, whether in words or images or any other human medium, any form of naturalism must be ruled out as at best inadequate and worst distorting. As we know, realistic painting and sculpture has for a long time been used by the church as a means of teaching. So have scientific models by teachers of science, as when some chemical compound is represented by one of those complex structures of coloured balls and inter-connecting rods. Nobody believes that, seen through a microscope, the stuff actually looks like that. If they do, they have been deceived by the model; their imagination has got stuck at a literal level of interpretation. A religious art that does nothing to help people get beyond this kind of literalism is not just useless; it is disastrous. Such naturalism is the basis of all kitsch, the attractiveness of which is that it offers to save people the trouble of exercising their own creative imagination.

This is not of course to say that no naturalistic art can express genuine religious feeling, only that such a style can tempt us with what look like easy answers when in truth no such answers are to be found. Nor can it simply be assumed that a style that on the surface makes no intelligible sense must necessarily be saying something profound. Nevertheless the abstract movement which began in the early years of this century does offer a great deal that was missing from a realism that by then had become quite exhausted. By presenting a picture of the world free from the surface detail by which we have grown habituated to recognize that world, an art of abstraction can challenge the mind of the observer to find for him or herself a reality beyond, or within, the world of appearances; in the language of mediaeval philosophy, to look beyond the accidents to find the substance. One of its greatest exponents observed: 'As I see it, painting and religious experience are the same thing, and what we are searching for is the understanding and realization of infinity.'[5] Many people still find it hard to see anything religious in Ben Nicholson's work, but its development over half a century is marvellously summed up in another remark of his: 'Realism has been abandoned in the search for reality; the principal objective of abstract art is precisely this reality.'[6]

Even more insidious than kitsch is a process that has, to my knowledge, no name but is even more destructive because what it starts with, and feeds upon, is the genuinely creative work of other people. I have already pointed out how hard, perhaps how impossible, it is for us today to experience the impact made by the great innovative artists or writers of the past on the men and women of their time. It is no great effort for us to appreciate Rembrandt, or so we think. We are astonished to read that his contemporaries saw so little in him. Did the Parisians of a century ago really feel that those first Impressionist landscapes were a travesty of nature? And did the London audiences of 1790 really think Haydn was a noisy composer? How little they knew! We experience these works

65

with eyes and ears that have grown accustomed to far tougher demands. What a relief to turn from Stockhausen back to Bach, from Samuel Beckett back to Sheridan, from Francis Bacon to Gainsborough. A relief: Yes, that is just it; it is a most welcome relaxation, to read, to see, to listen to something on which we don't have to work. This is nothing to feel guilty about, but we should be alert to what is happening. It is the same as what happens when a metaphor dies. What once could stir the imagination has now become part of the background to life, like that Mozart Piano Concerto you listened to while shaving this morning, or the Schubert Symphony you had with your *Guardian* and shredded wheat for breakfast. Nothing can actually turn Mozart into kitsch, but he or any other great composer or artist can become the equivalent for us once we get into the habit of treating their work with less than our full attention. It is a process that may be hard to counteract.[7] It will take something like that *metanoia* that is so inadequately translated in our gospels as repentance for such a reversal to be possible. Only then can we hope to recover the ability to appropriate such works at a depth that will be, for us, creative.

What is true of art, poetry and music is also true of ritual and the language of ritual. There are dangers, it must be recognized, in regarding ritual as a form of art. It can, in the hands of the ritualist, become an end in itself. (But then so can art, in the hands of the artist.) Nevertheless, if we can see ritual as essentially a means of communication, of sharing, the parallels between it and some of those other forms of language we have been looking at may throw light on all of them.

It is an essential characteristic of any true art, I have suggested, that it appeals to the freedom of those who, in whatever role, engage in it. How can this be true of ritual? Ritual, surely, is highly conventionalized; it allows little or no scope for individual expression. Those who participate in it are bound by its formal structures. How then can it be said to demand, or even allow, a free response? However if we look back to what was said earlier about the ways in which art and poetry communicate we may see how ritual can, like them, be a means of sharing, a shared expression of worship, and how it too, when it is working properly, makes possible a free growth of the spirit, and this because of, and not in spite of, the rules it obeys.

Consider a phrase commonly used in a dismissive sense, 'an empty ritual'. But perhaps this is an essential feature of all good ritual, to be empty. Just as the artists of our century have recovered something that should never have been missing from art, the trick of leaving space for us to fill with our experience, so ritual should always leave a certain space, a certain silence if you like, behind or within the words, which will welcome all those who take part to enter and be themselves. Ritual too needs to be appropriated, to be filled with a personal meaning by those who find in its very formality the freedom they are looking for. What then does all this tell us about the language proper to ritual?

First of all, that it will not be the language of the everyday exchange of information. That kind of language is too direct, too specific, like that realistic pseudo-art that allows of only one possible interpretation, demanding nothing of the imagination and not giving the individual freedom to relate it to his or her own experience or needs. In other words, the language of ritual must not, on the surface at least, too easily make sense. This does not mean a return to obscurity or meaninglessness for its own sake. What, however, it must not offer is the kind of sense that can be grasped without imagination. Such language will allow, and encourage, each participant to find meaning in it: his or her own meaning.

That of course is only one aspect of ritual language. This freedom will be one to foster not an out-and-out individualism but rather the opposite: a sharing in which each individual can make his or her own often unspoken contribution. What may seem to set everyone free to move on centrifugal paths of personal reflection can in fact act as a focus, bringing together a great diversity of thought and feeling. And this is where art and ritual can be seen to have most in common, because the work of art not only offers a kind of confirmation of individual experience, so that we can each one of us say 'yes' to it in personal contexts that will inevitably be quite different; it can also communicate an insight which will transcend any particular feeling we may bring to it, so that our own understanding is thereby enhanced or found to be inadequate; that initial 'yes' then becomes 'yes, I see'. Ritual can do something similar. As each of us may find in a single poetic image some resonance with our own condition, something that touches on our own immediate personal situation, so the language of the rite can bring together in an unspoken unity individuals who at the moment become aware of having each drawn insight from a common source.

We sometimes hear these days of the need to 'bring theology into the market place'. This curiously old-fashioned phrase does in fact apply only too well to some of the changes of ritual and liturgy which are on offer today. It is indeed the language of the supermarket and the information bureau that provides a model for many modern forms of worship: the literary equivalent of sliced loaves and fish-fingers, all pre-packed, hygienic, tasteless kitsch. In some cases the product is of such embarrassing banality that those who administer it feel bound to give some 'meaningfulness' to it by imposing their own personalities on it. This kind of expressionism still further infringes the freedom of others to participate at any real depth.

It may be of course that this is all part of the price we must pay for that egalitarianism which is the modern form of democracy. Market research will establish what flavours and what forms of packaging appeal to this or that percentage of customers. If the choice whether of art or of ritual is to be left to a majority vote in any society it is perhaps only to be expected that those forms will be preferred that make least demands on the understanding or the imagination. Unfortunately in the long-running controversy over new forms of liturgy the polarization has been between the champions of ancient poetry and those of modern prose. It is nothing less than tragic that those who have stood for renewal appear to have taken as their highest priority the literal intelligibility of all forms of worship. The resulting product, by freeing the worshipper from the need for any creative effort, is predictably lacking in the power either to express or to evoke an awareness of mystery.

* 7 *

The Mystery of Creation

I wrote earlier of the need to keep clear in our minds a distinction between the language of mystery and the mystery itself which that language tries to articulate. To do otherwise, I said, would be to abandon any claim to objectivity. It may be, of course, that no one can approach the mystery with detachment. Kierkegaard declared that truth was subjectivity. It was central to all the thinking of Martin Buber that the language of I-It must give way to that of I-Thou in the encounter with ultimate reality; that God could be spoken to but not about. Yet the whole history of European thought shows not so much that this is untrue as that the opposite is also true. And this is confirmed by common experience. The files of the Alister Hardy Research Centre are full of personal accounts from men and women of our time who had felt their lives affected by some power beyond themselves and wrote to describe its impact on them. There are great pressures on us today to believe that such experiences are 'all in the mind', or 'purely psychological'. (It is high time, incidentally, that the implications of that last phrase were exposed: the claim, that is, that there are certain experiences which need a psychologist to explain them, and that when this is done there is no more to be said.) Nothing is more characteristic of these accounts than their repeated insistence that such explanations will not do. It is worth noting that William James, who gave great importance to what he called 'the subconscious self' in his discussion of religious experience, never suggests that it is itself in any way the origin of such experience. So he writes:

> If there be higher spiritual agencies that can directly touch us, the psychological condition of their doing so might be our possession of a subconscious region which alone should yield access to them.

and again

> If the grace of God miraculously operates, it probably operates through the subliminal door. [1]

The overwhelming majority of the accounts in the files of the Hardy Centre would agree with this. Though they generally put it very differently, their writers are even more insistent than James that there is Something There. The problem then is one of language. Where the distinction between objective and subjective no longer applies, what forms of expression are there that belong neither to the world of fact nor simply to that of feeling?

A possible escape from this subjective-objective dicho-tomy, a way of having it both ways, may be to take a leaf out of an old grammar book. Learning Latin verbs you were taught first to divide them into two groups, the transitive and the intransitive. The transitive were those that 'took an object': that is, they could not meaningfully be used except in relation to some external thing or person. Such were 'to have' (a dog) or 'to take' (a biscuit). These objects you duly learnt to put in the accusative case. The intransitive verbs, in contrast, were those that were complete in themselves, as 'to sleep', or 'to prosper'; here no object was necessary, hence no accusative. All verbs fell into one or other of these two categories. Well, almost; but then there were examples that didn't quite fit into this neat division. 'To run', or 'to die': they looked intransitive enough, but what about 'to run a race', or 'to die a good death'? These nouns, they were not really objects; the race was not separate from the running, the death was all part of the dying. So they were called 'cognate accusatives', cognate meaning 'of the same nature as' the verbs they related to.

So here: when I speak of books or bicycles, these things are unquestionably external objects, and my language about them will be the plain language of objectivity. But the mysteries of my spiritual perception cannot be external in this same way; yet they are still, I am convinced, as real and independent of me as the race I run or the death I die. So the language I use of them can be described as cognate; it will in some way partake of the essential nature of those mysteries of which it attempts to speak. So in this no-man's-land where language and mystery meet we cannot practise the one in detachment from the other. Part at least of the mystery we try to articulate is that this identification is possible; that creation is at work in even the humblest, most insignificant attempt to describe the source of that creation.

We are all probably familiar with the idea of entropy. The water in the bath gets colder the longer you lie in it, until finally its temperature is the same as that of the air in the bathroom. Clocks run down unless they are wound up, batteries go flat unless they are recharged, sandcastles are flattened by the incoming tide. One day the sun itself will cool. The sum total of energy in the universe is limited, and it all tends everywhere to reach a dead level. We may think we can create new resources of energy. We cannot, except by drawing on existing resources elsewhere. The universe is a closed system. So states the second law of thermodynamics.

Much of our experience persuades us that this is inescapable.

> To think that two and two are four
>   And neither five nor three
> The heart of man has long been sore
>   And long 'tis like to be.[2]

But then we have one of those experiences that make us question Housman's despairing arithmetic: experiences that seem to wire us up to a world whose energy is subject to no such law and remains inexhaustible however much we draw upon it. William James was fond of using the word 'more', indeed 'a MORE', to indicate this unaccountable remainder. So he writes of what he calls 'the higher self' as being 'coterminous with a MORE of the same quality which is operative in the universe outside of him'.[3]

Five years after the Russian revolution of 1917 the painter Kasimir Malevich gave a public lecture in the town of Vitebsk.[4] It was his final appeal to the rulers of the new state to recognize that religion was not as they thought their enemy. In the beginning, he started – and it really does sound rather like the opening of St John's Gospel; perhaps he meant it to – the source of all life in society is energy, VOSBUZHDENYE, pure, absolute, unlimited, beyond time, beyond space, beyond any human calculation or comprehension. Pervading the whole universe, in humanity alone, he said, this energy reaches the level of consciousness; in our species alone (as Malevich quaintly puts it, inside the human skull) that energy expresses itself in concepts: concepts of infinity, of eternity, of perfection. And it is this insatiable search for 'forms of perfection' that is common to the artist, the industrialist and the theologian. So what, he asked, are we quarrelling about? Predictably, as we now realize, the new regime did not respond to this appeal.

It is significant that no totalitarian state has ever given its poets and artists freedom. Totalitarianism can never tolerate this vision of an unlimited source of energy. If the human heart really is restless until it finds its rest in an infinite reality, then no political or economic system, such as Marxism, that claims to be able ultimately to satisfy all the needs of its citizens is ever going to win their total allegiance. Such a society is never going to find the creative imagination anything but an enemy. The work of free spirits like Käthe Kollwitz or Solzhenitsyn will be a constant reminder that there are resources available to ordinary men and women that no secular state can provide: that the sum total of energy is not limited, and that we ourselves, every one of us, can add to it. (Pasternak's *Doctor Zhivago* is of course the classic text here.)

Creation is sometimes described as *ex nihilo*, out of nothing. That phrase can be very misleading, suggesting as it does some magical materialization out of thin air. But go back to Genesis. In the beginning the earth was without form and void; the brute matter, or primordial slime, was already there for God's creative ability to work on. What followed was a separation of the heaven from the earth, of the dry land from the waters, the shaping of raw material into the forms of nature we now see around us. So when Mozart writes a symphony, the notes, the paper they are written on, the instruments they are to be played by, are already there. When Henry Moore starts a sculpture, the stone is already there, had no doubt been there for quite a long time. All he had to do was to chip away a bit here and a bit more there: nothing magical about that. Yet we know there is more to be said than this. Mozart's *G Minor Symphony* or Moore's *Reclining Figure* are not simply the end results of putting certain marks on paper or chiselling stone into a certain shape. They cannot just be described as the effects, of which the writing or the carving were the causes. That on the other hand could be said of a table; for all the skill of the craftsman who made it, it is still no more than the sum of its parts. Even an electric light bulb, this marvellous transformation of common materials into a miracle of incandescent filament – even here the word creation is hardly appropriate.

Why not? The difference is that, for all its brilliance, this bulb is subject to the law of entropy. Not only does it depend on an external source of energy for its light; it will soon follow a thousand other defunct bulbs to some municipal rubbish dump, where no doubt there will be an old table or two to keep it company. But won't the same be true of your old Henry Moores in time? After all, the Egyptian Sphinx is no longer in very good shape. And what happened to the last two movements of Schubert's Unfinished Symphony? Perhaps they lighted the fire in some Viennese grate a century and a half ago. There's entropy for you. Of course all material objects have their day, however much care we spend on their preservation. But I have I hope said enough about works of art for it to be clear that the work done upon them, the work they do, the work they enable us to do, is not subject to any of those physical laws of change and decay. On the contrary, the real creation they achieve is the creation of energy.[5]

Can this be proved? Can it be measured? Of course it cannot. That is because this energy, this pure, absolute and unlimited VOSBUZHDENYE that Malevich saw as the source and sustainer of all life, is beyond all such calculation or measurement. The fact remains, though, that we, all of us, have been empowered, through this gift of creative imagination, to make our own contribution to this unlimited reserve of spiritual energy, and by doing so to enable our fellow men and women to do the same.

What form that contribution will take will be, in part at least, up to us. When Coleridge said 'We know a poet because he makes us poets', he was speaking as a poet himself; that was the form that POIESIS took in him. But who knows what it will do in other people?

We are shaken or lifted out of our ordinary state of consciousness. Many of our faculties are, for the moment enhanced. We feel keener perceptions coming into action within us. We are given more than our normal stock of penetrative sympathy. We feel that we can enter into people's feelings and understand the quality of their lives better than ever before. . . Some sort of mysterious liberation or empowerment seems to be approaching.[6]

A peak experience? A drug trip? No; just some reflections by a journalist of the 1920s, C. E. Montague, on the power of poetry. The effect of that power on different people will always be unpredictable. Yet popular opinion about this is hard to shift. It is difficult to persuade people that poetry is not just for poets any more than art is for artists, or at least that such activities are not the concern just of some intellectual or cultural élite, but that any work of the creative imagination is infinitely convertible into forms of energy far beyond the conception of the individual poet or artist, composer or dramatist, architect or choreographer who first produced it.

What might be called the convertibility of creative energy[7] is beautifully described by Christopher Alexander in his book, *The Timeless Way of Building*:

There is a central quality which is the root criterion of life and spirit in a man, a town, a building or a wilderness. This quality is objective and precise, but it cannot be named. . . The search which we make for this quality in our own lives is the central search of any person, and the crux of any individual person's story. It is the search for those moments and situations when we are most alive. . . We cannot be aware of these most precious moments when they are actually happening. Yet each of us knows from experience the feeling which this quality creates in us. Places which have this quality invite this quality to come to life in us. And when we have this quality in us, we tend to make it come to life in towns and buildings which we help to build. It is a self-supporting, self-maintaining, generating quality. It is the quality of life. And we must seek it, for our own sakes, in our surroundings, simply in order that we ourselves can become alive.[8]

Architecture is of all the arts perhaps the one that makes the widest and most immediate impact on any society, its aim being to create or at least to help shape a whole environment. Yet what Alexander writes of here is true of all arts which are genuinely creative; they will all, in his words, 'invite this quality to come to life in us'. Note that it is only an invitation: the response must still be ours.

All this should remind us not to underrate our own capacity for POIESIS, in whatever field our gifts may lie. There is no knowing what they may lead to, even in those – especially in those – with whom we may feel we have little or nothing in common.

* 8 *

Theology and Childhood

Those without poetry: their source of innocence lost.
Theodore Roethke[1]

It may seem presumptuous of me to have written at such length on this subject without considering the claims of theology to have something to say about it. It will I hope have been noticed that I, being no theologian, have tried all along to confine my discussion to the question, 'In what language should we attempt to speak about the mystery?' rather than offer an answer to the question, 'What is the mystery about which we are trying to speak?' But, as has at various points become apparent, the two questions cannot always be kept apart. The language and the mystery are cognate. Examine the language, even better, practise the language, and in doing so you will learn something about the mystery. So what can theology say about all this?

It has often been observed that the literary history of any culture always begins with poetry, and that the writing of prose comes much later. Eventually the two modes become quite distinct. So history becomes a discipline with standards and criteria of its own and only occasionally looks back over its shoulder to the tradition of epic or ballad from which it long ago originated. What about theology? Here too is a genre of prose-writing that has developed on lines of its own. But can it, should it, so easily turn its back on its ancestral origins in drama, poetry and mythology?

'Our birth', wrote Wordsworth, 'is but a sleep and a forgetting.' What I would with great diffidence suggest is that if theology does ever quite forget its own prenatal visions it will have lost much of its own *raison d'être*. So far from putting its own childhood behind it theology must surely do all it can not to lose touch with it. All Christian theologians will of course be conscious of their need to be constantly returning to the historical roots of their faith; but what I mean is something more than this. In an earlier book[2] I tried to illustrate what it may mean for a person to keep such a link with his or her childhood – childhood being conceived of not as a period of immaturity to be grown out of but rather as an essential element in the growing human being, to be preserved and integrated into the mature adult personality. Christians in particular have ample authority for valuing the spiritual potential of childhood, and if we are really concerned to keep the child alive within ourselves we cannot limit our liabilities. There is no aspect of the whole theological enterprise that is exempt from this demand.

This will not mean that theologians should stop writing prose, any more than the preservation of an inner childhood in adult life will require a reversion to childish ways of thought or expression. A little earlier on I mentioned a certain loss of simplicity, and the work that is entailed in any attempt to recover it. To believe that such recovery is possible is surely the heart of the matter. When Roethke spoke of those without poetry as having lost their source of innocence he had an eye, no doubt, like Coleridge, to his own particular craft. But his belief in a simplicity still open to those who have eyes to see and ears to hear is one that we can all share, and act upon, not least those whose theology is avowedly an exploration of that one creative source.

It is one of the most disappointing aspects of modern educational philosophy that an obsession with developmental theory has obscured any vision of the unpredictable spirit of creation. Piaget and Erikson, Kohlberg and Fowler – they have all given faithful service to a culture that sees the child as an inefficient adult and requires a dependable technique for enabling it to become an efficient one. This psychology sees life in terms of tenure. What use is an education that does not equip the individual to come to grips with life? So beginning with a descriptive analysis of the stages of cognitive growth, these system-builders end up by presenting, or at least implying, a prescriptive framework within which young people may be taught to develop those faculties which will enable them to control, to manipulate, not to be at the mercy of, their circumstances; not to let them get out of hand but to master them. But tenure works both ways. We may have a grip on life; life may equally have a grip on us. Possessiveness leads to possession. Catelepsy is the medical term for such a seizure, when freedom of movement, even consciousness itself may be lost. The word has the same root as that used by the writer of the Fourth Gospel to describe the mastery that the darkness could never achieve over that light that came into the world; as the old translation says, it did not comprehend it.

This mode of educational thought is of course a direct product of a competitive society which measures success in terms of its exploitation and control of the environment, both material and human. But there is a high price to pay. I spoke earlier on of the immunity we may acquire to the impact of works of the creative imagination. This is no other than that 'paucity that never was simplicity' of Wilfred Owen's battle-hardened soldiers. They had become, as our education may lead us to become, immune to that mystery which lies 'beyond the last seas and the hapless stars'. The artist, on the other hand, the poet, the fully creative human being, these are the ones who have never, or never quite, acquired that immunity. They will always be at risk. This the world may see as a deficiency. It could not be more wrong. The one really fatal disease that may finally destroy our humanity is the loss of that openness to the creative spirit, and its replacement with the belief that the whole of life can ultimately be brought under our control. Amid the (rightly) unending discussions on the aims of education nothing is surely more urgent than the diagnosis, and prevention, of this (as it might be called) Acquired Immunity to Mystery Syndrome. So the developmentalists may well be accurate in their observations; but the more important question is how far they are right in what they choose to observe; what light, that is, their narrow beam throws on our understanding of humanity in its full, its infinite potential. What they are in danger of ignoring, particularly when they speak of religion or morality or faith, is that there is no predictable or automatic evolution in the growth of that one element in every one of us that can make spiritual, as distinct from intellectual or physical, life an effective, operational reality. In this respect it may well be asked whether the impressive contributions of this branch of psychology represent any real advance on the understanding of Nicodemus ('You, a teacher in Israel and you do not know these things!'; John 3. 10) who had to be reminded that the wind of the spirit would blow where it pleased, and that no one could tell where it came from or where it would go.

A child has a picture of human existence peculiar to himself, which he probably never remembers after he has lost it: the original vision of the world. . . Certain dreams convince me that a child has this vision, in which there is a completer harmony of all things with each other than he will ever know again.[3]

'Certain dreams': no one in the literature of this century has expressed more poignantly than Muir the loss of Eden.[4] Yet what he invites us to share is not just self-pity; those dreams led him not to the self-indulgence of nostalgia but to a conviction that the original vision need not in fact be totally lost, even though it may never be recovered in its original form. As we all know, nothing is easier to sentimentalize than childhood. It would be quite wrong simply to identify childhood with creativity (a word incidentally that needs a far more precise definition than it usually gets if it is to be allowed into responsible debate on this subject), as it would be to identify spirituality with the imagination. Imagination is the faculty by which our innate potential for spirituality can be brought to flower. Childhood, as here conceived, is just another name for that same spiritual potential in each of us. Those who speak of it as something holy are right, but only if they will see it as the seed, the embryo, the root – any of these organic metaphors will do if they remind us that the life that may grow from it is likely to take a shape quite unrecognizable from the form in which we first knew it.

It is not for nothing that we have two different words, 'childlike' and 'childish', to distinguish between those whose childhood has been enabled to grow and take its proper place in the adult personality and those in whom it has not. Milton was speaking of his blindness when he wrote of 'that one talent which 'tis death to hide lodged with me useless'. His words could well be taken as a warning to all those engaged in any aspect of religious education of the terrible consequences of a childhood that has been allowed to become stunted or even atrophied. Earlier on I compared spirituality with sexuality, each being a natural aspect of our human make-up. The parallel could be taken further. Just as sexuality may remain inactive long after physical maturity has been reached – many adults have felt its first real stirrings quite late in life – so with our spirituality. Given the kind of education that is standard in our secularized system, with perhaps the additional inoculation against religion provided by compulsory church attendance, it is hardly surprising that large numbers of young and not-so-young people today show all the symptoms of a totally undeveloped or even pathological spirituality. Something almost akin to seduction may then be necessary if that dormant spirituality is to be activated. Does that constitute an improper suggestion? But why should a secular, materialist culture always expect us to play by its own rules? Perhaps it needs to be hit below the belt if we are to loose its hold upon us. We are fortunate to live in a culture still rich in such potential means of seduction – by which of course I mean a still living tradition of the arts in all their creative variety. Despite this, however, most of us are in fact resigned to our loss of childhood. Like Nicodemus we find the return to that primal simplicity impossible to contemplate. We cannot turn back the years. In a literal sense we are quite right. Yet that wind still blows where it will, and to those who are open to it nothing is irreversible.

Nothing irreversible? No. But there is one condition. We have it on the highest authority that it is possible to reach a point of no return. In discussing revelation, I pointed out how throughout the Western world the name of Christ is commonly used without any trace of reverence; a practice which causes distress to many who find in the figure of Jesus an inspiration and a model for their own spiritual growth. I will not say such distress is groundless; but those who feel strongly about this devaluation, as they may see it, of what they regard as sacred should take comfort from some of Jesus' own recorded words. Speaking ill of the Son of Man, he said, was forgivable. So it does not matter all that much if you get your christology wrong, and as for all the mindless expletives that litter the language, well, there are far more serious things to think about. Sin against the Spirit, for instance. For that, this same passage tells us, there can be no forgiveness, either in this world or the next. It makes sense. Let your batteries go dead and you will not get a word out of your transistor, not a note, not a bleep. Cut yourself off from the Spirit and there is no way, humanly speaking, that the divine creative energy is ever going to get through to you. It is not up to us, of course, to lay down what forms that mysterious initiative may take. Grass can grow through the tarmac. With the Spirit at work, anything can happen, and probably will. But it surely is up to us to keep our receivers in good order and not wilfully to bring about that state of emergency in which normal lines of communication have to be by-passed and rescue will have to come, if it comes at all, by means that are quite beyond us. It may be little consolation to reflect that that is how the Spirit usually does have to get through to us in the end. Its workings will almost always take strange and unfamiliar forms, and the best that most of us can hope for is not too often to be found in opposition to it. One thing we can do; we can do our best to keep our creative imagination in good practice. And this is what the work of art is all about: that work which is art, that work which we can all in our different ways practise and become a little better at, and so when the time comes be a little less likely to be caught without any language in which to witness to that hope that can so easily die in solitude. No one has summed this up better than Wallace Stevens:

> The wonder and mystery of art, as indeed of religion in the last resort, is the revelation of something wholly 'other' by which the inexpressible loneliness of thinking is broken and enriched. [5]

* 9 *

Personal Postscript

In one of her most intriguing stories Isak Dinesen tells of a man who by the accident of birth (he was the one survivor of twin boys) has lived his life uncertain whether his destiny was to be a priest or an artist. He comes to find some assurance in the reflection that there is not after all so much difference between the two. One of the things, he says, they have in common is that each 'is placed, in his life on earth, with his back to God and his face to man'.[1] What can this possibly mean?

I have already mentioned (pp. 39f.) the dangers or perplexities that may arise when art becomes a sort of substitute for religion, and the unhealthy consequences for society that may result. For the creative individual who is genuinely trying to hold on to the purity of his or her own vision this unbalanced reception may be seriously disorienting, quite apart from the possible financial pressures or temptations. More often of course the person who really has something to say will never get a hearing at all. It is hard to say which of these extreme responses makes it more difficult for artists to go on believing in themselves not as servants of some higher aesthetic ideal, let alone as creators of investment commodities or as entertainers, but simply as people who have some insight to share and long to be met on their own ground by others who will accept them as equals.

As equals? Yes, because it is this ground of common humanity that is also the ground of any authority that the visionary can claim. There are all kinds of authority that society accustoms us to accept, but in the last resort the only kind that really matters is that which we recognize in the person who has done, or known, or understood, something that we have not; has been somewhere that we have not. Of course a vast amount of what we think we 'know' is taken on someone else's authority; life would be impossible if we had to prove everything for ourselves. But it must be clear by now that at the level on which the language of mystery is spoken there can be no question of taking anyone else's word for anything. Why after all do we speak of 'recognizing' someone as an authority? To recognize is to know from previous acquaintance. How come, then, that we recognize authority in *King Lear*, in *Cancer Ward*, in the *Glagolitic Mass*? Not because of any previous experience we have of ancient Britain, of the Soviet Camps, of Bohemian folk music, but because at the deeper level of our common humanity Shakespeare and Solzhenitsyn and Janacek all speak to us of something we already know, however dimly. Somewhere inside us an echo, a resonance is stirred; something in each of us says 'yes'. If these figures speak with authority it is because they are like us, in sharing our humanity, yet also unlike, in having something that we want, something we can use, something we can appropriate, something that could perhaps help us to become the people we have it in us to become. Then each of us may, in some small degree, become an authority, not by copying someone else but by doing the same kind of work on our own lives. Each of us in our own quite different ways may become a person who has done, or known, or understood; who has been there, and come back to tell the tale.

Now perhaps we can begin to find meaning in what Isak Dinesen's character is talking about. To have spiritual authority is to have been there for oneself, and to have come back. The point is not, most emphatically, that we can employ either the priest or the artist to do something on our behalf, to save ourselves the trouble. Quite the contrary, what they can do, all they can do, is show, first, that it is possible, and then, that the journey, that transcendence, is required of us all. We may put it off for as long as we like; we may put it off for a lifetime. Or we may have a go at it straight away – and then really begin to live, to discover our own lives, to explore that ocean that (we now find) touches all that we do.

I have mentioned the kind of false humility that prevents us believing in our own creative imagination – or gives us a pretext for denying it. This evasion is in part a consequence of that inflation of art into a mystique. What? Me an artist? To have a healthy belief in one's own potential authority becomes a near-impossibility in a culture whose values are so distorted. Yet it is only by accepting that responsibility that one can discover that the claim it implies is not after all so arrogant, so outrageous. It is no more than a claim to be a human being – that species of animal that alone is able to conceive of the world being different from the way it is.

In discussing the enemies of art I put imitation first, having in mind the kind of realistic representationalism that is still the only artistic ideal that many people can comprehend. But imitation can take other and more insidious forms. If you believe the world is simply a battleground of conflicting forces and so a pretty nasty place, that men and women are at heart basically unpleasant creatures whose occasional good behaviour to one another is motivated only by fear or greed, and that it is self-deception or hypocrisy to offer any other view of life, then your art, your drama, your literature, your

87

music will probably be praised today for its realism, its objectivity, honesty, sincerity and so forth. One fashionable artist in particular, whose inventive mastery of painting technique is beyond question, has made his considerable reputation (and fortune) by portraying his fellow men and women in a state of advanced decomposition and corruption, physical and spiritual. If you ask what is the value of this portrayal of human degradation, the answer comes quickly: it is the truth. The artist is simply painting what he sees – and what you would see too if your eyes were open: this is what the world has come to; this is what we are all like under the skin. The same 'truth' is offered by a whole genre of literature and television drama: the best that can be said for life is that little good can be said for it. This argument for a pyschological, as distinct from a photographic, realism should deceive us no more than any other justification of art as that which holds up a mirror to nature. This is, once more, to reduce the creative imagination to the status of fantasy; to refuse to see any value in that essentially human capacity for seeing things other than the way they are.

This, though, raises another question. If it is not enough for the artist simply to reflect the state of the world as he or she sees it, if with the gift of creative imagination goes also some obligation to be open to some new vision of what that world might be, is one not in danger of confusing art with moralism? No so: the essential difference is that the moralist knows all too clearly what changes are desirable, while the artist remains open to the spirit from whatever direction it may blow. The creative impulse is not to be harnessed to a moral programme. Nor, come to that, to a religious mission. There is a terrible certainty in some of the proclamations of orthodoxy that can strike chill into the heart. How can anyone speak with such assurance about the mystery? Which brings me back to Isak Dinesen.

There is one last question which his interrogator puts to that Janus-figure of hers. (He is in fact a Cardinal, a prince of the church.) 'I understand . . . that you are a loyal and incorrupt-ible servant. I feel that the Master whom you serve is very great. Yet are you sure that it is God whom you serve?' To which the Cardinal replies: 'That, Madame, is a risk which the artists and the priests of the world have to run.'

There will be some, perhaps the majority of those who have persevered this far with this book, to whom this will be a quite unsatisfactory conclusion. What kind of religion is it that cannot, at the heart of its teaching, offer any such certainty? Have we really got to live with the possibility that all our hopes, all our aspirations, are built on a delusion? Ah, but that is not the same question. To be deluded is to take one kind of reality for another: a dream for a memory of waking life, plastic roses for real roses. Only those who think they know can be deluded. The only certainty that any religion can offer, or rather, that any religion should offer, is the certainty of Tertullian, who declared that he believed because it was impossible.[2] And it is that impossibility of belief that should be our starting point today. To whom are we to turn to help us believe the unbelievable?[3]

There are those who will tell us that we should start by getting free of our delusions; that we should be grateful to those who show us how things really are: those writers and artists, for example, who rub our noses in the decomposing squalor of humanity. Like alcoholics who can have no hope of cure until they have hit the bottom and know it, perhaps we all need to have the reality of our condition brought home to us. But what is the reality? Is it truly the static dissolution, the frustration of all effort by the natural processes of decay, the omega-point of entropy? Or is it rather the infinite potential for re-creation in each and every one of us who is open to that *Creator Spiritus*? If the second, then the only question that matters is this: how can we recover, how can we help each other to recover, the capacity for believing the unbelievable? In a culture in which the language of a materialistic secularism has almost entirely replaced the language of religion the prospects may look dark. The opposite is surely true. If the traditional language of spirituality is, if not taboo, then at least for growing numbers of people no longer a credible option, the opportunities are infinitely expanded. If the energies of our spirituality are no longer confined to conventionally religious channels there is no limit to where they may appear. They are liable to leak out all over the place. Like some powerful but beneficent virus escaped from the laboratory, there is no knowing what part of our life may not suddenly be infected by them. Are we ready for this? Can we say, with David Jones, 'I have been on my guard not to condemn the unfamiliar'? He continues, 'For it is easy to miss Him at the turn of a civilization.'[4]

There are those who still find in traditional forms a quite satisfactory 'language', verbal or non-verbal, in which the mystery can be expressed and shared as a living reality. They may even ask what all the fuss is about. They may be content to see things continue pretty much the way they are. Yet all the evidence is that they are a fast-diminishing minority. I have called these final reflections a personal postscript. Others may look for the renewal of our spiritual tradition in quite different directions. My own feelings are best summed up by some remarks of Nicholas Wolterstorff's: words to which many will surely respond. He is speaking of those who protest against the elevation of the arts into a quasi-mystical cult. With this protest he agrees. But, he continues,

I am also persuaded that if, in their own vision of human existence, they fail to give adequate place to the artistic heritage of mankind, to this flowering of our creaturely potential, they will over and over drive people away from their religions. For there are those who cannot say no to the arts of mankind. There are those whose nature respond deeply to this heritage that if forced, by the spokesmen of the religion in which they have been reared, to choose, they will, with sorrow, suffering and anger, depart from home to a far country.[5]

Notes

NOTES

1 Mystery and Imagination

1. Richard Wilbur, 'For Dudley', in *Walking to Sleep*, Faber 1971, p. 25.

2. Thus Petru Dumitriu, after quoting Wittgenstein's 'whereof one cannot speak thereof one must be silent', asks: 'To whom shall I address my silence?' (Petru Dumitriu, *To the Unknown God*, Collins 1982, p. 123).

3. John Dewey has a fine image to emphasize this point:

A primary task is thus imposed upon one who undertakes to write upon the philosophy of the fine arts. This task is to restore continuity between the refined and intensified forms of experience that are works of art and the everyday events, doing and sufferings that are universally recognized to constitute experience. Mountain peaks do not float unsupported; they do not even just rest upon the earth. They are the earth in one of its manifest operations (John Dewey, *Art as Experience*, Putnam, NY 1934, p. 3).

4. It may be instructive to compare this example of what I would call a creative conversation with some other kinds of dialogue. Some psychologists use the term 'clinical interview' to describe the kind of question and answer process that is designed to elicit from the 'subject' (meaning the person being studied) objective data relating to his or her views, attitudes, beliefs and so forth about a specific area of life. Such a conversation is not designed, in fact it would be rejected as unscientific if it attempted, to alter those views, attitudes etc. or to bring about any change in the person under investigation. An interview of this kind may well yield useful information, but there is always the danger that the presuppositions of the investigator will have priority over any open-minded concern for what the other person is trying to say. His or her responses will not be free: they will be required to conform to the specifications for the research programme. How often is the man or woman who is subjected to this kind of inquisition prompted to say, 'That's not how I would put the question', or 'Yes, but if you look at it another way . . .' To be open to look at things another way, and to allow the other to do the same, is the first condition of any creative dialogue.

Very different is the kind of dialogue that occurs in what might be called the exhibition interview. In its most typical and blatant form it is commonly to be seen on television, when some prominent personality is fed with the sort of questions that will enable him or her to present a self-portrait appropriate to the occasion. Dialogue is hardly the word for this kind of confrontation. In contrast to the clinical interview, here the role of the interviewer is to be totally subordinate to the subject of the 'portrait'. This is so even when the questions put are probing, aggressive or in other ways framed to put pressure on the man or woman being interviewed to reveal more than he or she might have to a more compliant or sycophantic interviewer.

What prevents each of these kinds of interview from being humanly creative is the inequality of both, or all, those involved. For a much healthier picture of creative conversation see Jung's description of the ideal relationship between analyst and client (in *Modern Man in Search of a Soul*, Routledge and Kegan Paul 1933, pp. 58ff.). There he insists on the need for each of the participants in the analytic situation to be equally open to learn from, and be changed by, the other.

5. Seamus Heaney, *Death of a Naturalist*, Faber 1966, p. 18.

2 Imagination and Fantasy

1. Boris Pasternak, letter to Jacqueline de Proyard, 1959; quoted in Guy De Mallac, *Boris Pasternak, his Life and Art*, Souvenir Press 1983, p. 344.

2. The distinction made here between imagination and fantasy is of course much the same as that made by Coleridge between imagination and fancy, the latter being 'no other than a mode of memory emancipated from the order of time and space', with 'all its materials ready made from the law of association', while the imagination is 'a repetition in the finite mind of the eternal act of creation in the infinite I AM'. (That to Coleridge was the 'primary imagination', the 'secondary' differing from it 'only in degree and in the mode of its operation'.) For his full account see *Biographia Literaria*, Chapter 13. A useful survey of the history of these ideas is to be found in R. C. Brett, *Fancy and Imagination*, Methuen 1969, especially in Chapter 2.

See also Keats' remark about Coleridge, quoted in the note below.

3. This is of course what Keats described as 'negative capability': 'That is, when a man is capable of being in uncertainties, mysteries, doubts, without any irritable reaching after fact and reason.' He goes on to criticize Coleridge for 'being incapable of remaining content with half-knowledge' (Letter to G. & T. Keats, 21 December 1817).

Carla Needleman describes the same need in the context of the potter's experience:

> The need for positive results is so much a part of our way of life, the attitude of the achiever is so fixed in us, that we scarcely can envision a different way of life. We stand in so peculiar a relationship to results that the products of our own hands bring about a confusion in us. We need to know, right away, whether they are good or bad; we need to know, to pin down, to decide, so that we will know how to feel. The fact of our lives is uncertainty, and we crave certainty. The fact of our lives is change, movement, and we long for 'arriving' . . . I am not suggesting that this attitude towards results is the only attitude conditioning the way a craftsman works, or even that this attitude can be, or is, obvious to me every time I sit down at the wheel . . . I do suggest that the desire to succeed is the progenitor of real failure and that this attitude is a far more subtly pervasive force than we realize. . . The craving for results in objects, or in opinions, the need to

name, the need to 'know', which means to end the discomfort of not knowing, is the seemingly innocuous backdrop against which all our activities take place (Carla Needleman, *The Work of Craft*, Avon Books, NY 1981, pp. 3, 6).

4. Edward FitzGerald, *The Rubaiyat of Omar Khayyam*.

5. Heidegger's passionate protest against the grip of technological thought on modern society illustrates such an addiction, 'mere willing' being the driving force that powers every form of fantasy.

What is deadly is not the much-discussed atomic bomb as this particular death-dealing machine. What has long since been threatening man with death, and indeed with the death of his own nature, is the unconditional character of mere willing in the sense of purposeful self-assertion in everything. What threatens man in his very nature is the willed view that man, by the peaceful release, transformation, storage and channelling of the energies of physical nature, could render the human condition tolerable for everybody and happy in all respects. . . The essence of technology comes to the light of day only slowly. This day is the world's night, rearranged into merely technological day. This day is the shortest day. It threatens a single endless winter. Not only does protection now withhold itself from man, but the integralness of the whole of what is remains now in darkness. The world becomes without healing, unholy. Not only does the holy, as the track to the godhead, thereby remain concealed; even the tract to the holy, the hale and the whole, seems to be effaced. That is, unless there are still some mortals capable of seeing the threat of the unhealable, the unholy, as such (Martin Heidegger, *Poetry, Language, Thought*, Harper and Row 1975, pp. 116f.).

Those who are 'still capable of seeing the threat' are of course the poets, 'whose song turns our unprotected being into the Open and . . . sing the healing whole in the midst of the unholy' (ibid., p. 140).

6. So Lynn Ross-Bryant:
When we look at the world through the eyes of possibility we discover a place in which newness and spontaneity dominate. What is is not determinative of what might be. We are invited to create something new, and with each creation a myriad of new possibilities for creation come into being. Our imagination and expectations are altered with each new achievement.

The horizon of possibility is continually inviting us to move forward to new imaginings and new creations (Lynn Ross-Bryant, *Imagination and the Life of the Spirit*, Scholars Press, California 1981, p. 94).

7. If Wallace Stevens reserves this role for the poet it is only because he or she possesses in the most potent degree a capacity we all share for these 'supreme fictions'.

There is . . . a world of poetry indistinguishable from the world in which we live, or, I ought to say, no doubt, from the world in which we shall come to live, since what makes the poet the potent figure that he is, or was, or ought to be, is that he creates the world to which we turn incessantly and without knowing it and that he gives to life the supreme fictions without which we are unable to conceive of it (Wallace Stevens, *The Necessary Angel*, Random House, NY 1951, p. 31).

8. Thomas Hobbes, *The Leviathan*, Chapter 13 (p. 65 in the Dent, Everyman edition).

9. George Bernard Shaw, *Saint Joan*, Scene 1.

10. Thus he writes:

Hence I observe how needful it is for me to enter into the darkness, and to admit the coincidence of opposites, beyond all the grasp of reason, and there to seek the truth where impossibility meeteth me. And beyond that, beyond even the highest ascent of intellect, when I shall have attained unto that which is unknown to every intellect, and which every intellect judgeth to be most far removed from truth, there, my God, art Thou, who art Absolute Necessity. And the more that dark impossibility is recognized as dark and impossible, the more truly doth His Necessity shine forth, and is more unveiledly present. . . . Impossibility coincideth with necessity, and I have learnt that the place wherein Thou art found unveiled is girt round with the coincidence of contradictories, and this is the wall of Paradise wherein Thou dost abide. . . . Thus 'tis beyond the coincidence of contradictories that Thou mayest be seen, and nowhere this side thereof (Nicholas of Cusa, b. 1401, *The Vision of God*, Frederick Ungar, NY 1960, pp. 43f.).

11. Compare Rilke's idea of the 'Open', as set out in a letter relating to the eighth of his Duino Elegies:

> You must understand the concept of the 'Open', which I have
> tried to propose in the Elegy, in such a way that the animal's
> degree of consciousness sets it into the world without the animal's
> placing the world over against itself at every moment (as we do);
> the animal is in the world; we stand before it by virtue of that
> peculiar turn and intensification which our consciousness has
> taken.

He goes on to speak of

> that indescribably open freedom which perhaps has its (extremely
> fleeting) equivalents among us only in those first moments of love
> when one human being sees his own vastness in another, his
> beloved, and in man's elevation toward God (Rilke, letter of 25
> February 1926, quoted in Heidegger, *Poetry, Language, Thought*,
> p. 108).

The wider, indeed universal, implications of this openness are
described by John Taylor in terms of 'presence':

> 'Compassion' is the final operative word to define what the
> way of presence really means. It sums up the listening,
> responsive, agonizing receptivity of the prophet and the poet.
> For it is impossible to be open and sensitive in one direction
> without being open to all. If a man would open his heart
> towards his fellow he must keep it open to all other comers – to
> the stranger, to the dead, to the enchanting and awful presences
> of nature, to powers of beauty and terror, to the pain and
> anxiety of men, to the menace and catastrophe of our time, and
> to the overwhelming presence of God. . . . To present oneself
> to God means to expose oneself, in an intense and vulnerable
> awareness, not only to him but to all that is. And this is what,
> apart from Christ, we dare not do. Presence is too much for us
> to face (John Taylor, *The Primal Vision*, SCM Press 1963, pp.
> 191f.).

12. The point is one that William Blake never tired of making:
'What is it sets Homer, Virgil and Milton in so high a rank of art?
Why is the Bible more entertaining and instructive than any other
book? Is it not because they are addressed to the imagination,
which is spiritual sensation, and but mediately to the understanding or reason?' (Letter to Dr Trusler, 23 August 1799; in Geoffrey
Keynes (ed), *Blake's Poetry and Prose*, Nonesuch Library 1961,

p. 835.

13. I am grateful to Mr David Hay, Director of the Alister Hardy Research Centre, for permission to quote from these letters.

3   Tradition and the Work of Art

1. Cf. S. Giedion:

Today the common denominator in creed and ritual that once linked man to man has lost its force. Whereas in primitive eras magic, myth and religion provided man with a spiritual armor against a hostile environment, today he stands stripped and naked. . . Today the average man appears to have lost the key to his own being, even though he still believes that he knows what he likes and can express what he feels. . . The decline in our community life, our helplessness in finding forms for celebration of leisure, our lack of imaginative power to develop forms to counteract the maladies of our culture all indicate the extent of man's present disorientation (S. Giedion, *The Eternal Present*, The Bollington Foundation, NY 1962, p. 80).

2. Mary C. Richards, *Centering*, Wesleyan University Press, Middleton, Connecticut 1964, p. 112.

3. The word most commonly used by theologians for the study of those principles by which revelation is to be interpreted is 'hermeneutics'. There is an irony not always appreciated by Christians in this choice of a word derived from the name of a pagan god for the study of their scriptures. Hermes was the most unpredictable of all the Greek pantheon, being the god not only of travellers but also of practical jokers. As the messenger of all the other gods, he became known as the god of luck – you could not always be sure which particular god had sent you this piece of good fortune. So a stroke of luck was known as a 'hermeion', a gift from Hermes. Later he became associated with mystery religions and so with divination; hence the use of the modern word 'hermeneutic' for the interpretation of divine mysteries. It should not be hard to see in the strange history of this word some hint of the importance of the open imagination in the study of a 'revealed religion'.

Those who wish to analyse further the role of the imagination in the interpretation of scripture may find help in the fourfold scheme developed by John Cassian and St Bonaventure, and later used by Dante. According to this there were four levels at which any biblical text could be interpreted. At the *literal* level it could be taken as a record of simple fact or instruction. From this one could go on to interpret it at the *allegorical* level; here each element in the text could be understood as standing for something else, as in the interpretation of Christ's parable of the sower given in Matt. 13.28ff. The third level was the *moral*, at which the text could yield a meaning of particular relevance to the reader's own situation; this could also be described as the personal level. The fourth and highest was the *anagogical* or mystical level. To interpret scripture at this level meant to open oneself up to all the infinite meanings that its words might have for you, meanings that might well transcend the comprehension of any single individual. It was the level of ANAGOGE, that leading up of the spirit to new possibilities of understanding. It is not only the Bible, of course, to which these principles of interpretation may be applied.

4. John Milton, *Paradise Lost*, Book III, 42.

5. Carla Needleman has some pertinent things to say about this:

The earliest impressions in life, before the dominant role of speech, were impressed on a clean photographic plate, are the strongest, and underline all succeeding images. These came in through the body – light and dark, smell, sound, touch, shape, movement through space . . . and others, more subtle, for which we have no names. . . These impressions have intrinsic meaning – as sensations of the body. Perhaps the unconscious is merely a modern formulation; perhaps it is the consciousness of the body . . . become inaccessible to us by direct means because of the superimposed consciousness of the formulating mind. The great attraction of art, design, form is the wish within us to return to direct perception. The search by the artist for forms, lines, shapes that are true has to do with the great pleasure in turning back toward oneself, in self-reference, in listening for what is real in myself, looking for it, and observing with great joy that inside myself there is truth and the means for approaching it. . . We respond to a shape (colour, size, direction of movement) with the body. It resonates in the body directly, although the appreciation of the perception may be blocked by thought (*The Work of Craft*, pp. 23ff.).

6. A perceptive critic once said of Michael Tippett's Fourth Symphony: 'He works within the tradition but shatters the *status quo*' (Michael Hall in *Radio Times*, London, 4 September 1978).

7. John Berger, *Permanent Red*, Methuen 1960, p. 104.

8. Naum Gabo, letter to Herbert Read (1942), published in *Horizon*, Vol. 10, No. 53 (London, July 1944). The essentially communicative nature of the work of art is well brought out in this exchange between Pierre Soulages and Bernard Ceysson. Soulages says:

> I have never thought that painting could be reduced to its material aspects. The reality of a work is the threefold relationship that is established between the painting as object, the painter who produced it, and the person looking at it. And here all that has gone to make up those two people is involved: their past life history – everything about them, their sensitivity, personality and so on (Bernard Ceysson, *Soulages*, Bonfini Press 1980, p. 81).

9. Bridget Riley, in a paper given to the International Symposium on the Conservation of Contemporary Art in the National Gallery of Canada, July 1980, published in *Art Monthly*, No. 39, 1980, pp. 5, 9. A similar point is made by Merleau-Ponty:

> The painter can do no more than construct an image. He must wait for this image to come to life for other people. When he does, the work of art will have united these separate lives. . . It will dwell undivided in several minds, with a claim on every possible mind like a perennial acquisition (M. Merleau-Ponty, *Sense and Non-sense*, North Western University Press, Chicago 1964, p. 20).

10. Here are his actual words:

> A picture lives by companionship, expanding and quickening in the eyes of the sensitive observer. It dies by the same token. It is therefore a risky and unfeeling act to send it out into the world. How often it must be permanently impaired by the eyes of the vulgar and the cruelty of the impotent who would extend their affliction universally (Mark Rothko, 'The Ides of Art', in *Tiger's Eye 2*, New York, December 1944, p. 44).

11. A quotation, if indeed it is such, familiar to me since my schooldays. I have never been able to trace its source.

12. Anne Truitt, *Daybook*, Pantheon Books, NY 1982, p. 44.

13. Peter Fuller puts it well:

> Fine artists find they have been granted every freedom except the only one without which the others count as nothing: the freedom to act socially. It is only a mild exaggeration to say that no-one wants Fine Artists, except Fine Artists, and that neither they nor

anyone else have the slightest idea what they should be doing, or for whom they should be doing it. . . It is possible to say that a major infringement of the freedom of the artist at the moment is his lack of a genuine social function (Peter Fuller, *Beyond the Crisis in Art*, Readers and Writers Co-operative, London 1980, pp. 45f.).

14. For an excellent discussion of this topic see Nicholas Wolterstorff's article 'Art, Religion and the Elite' in Diane Apostolos-Cappadona (ed), *Art, Creativity and the Sacred*, Crossroad, NY 1985, pp. 262ff.

15. A suggestive parallel is offered by James Varigu:

We know that iron particles in a magnetic field will react to the magnetic field in such a way as to become themselves magnetized by induction. That is, they become little magnets which then generate their own microscopic magnetic field, and attract or repel one another. . . . But for the iron particles themselves to become magnetized, some of the energy of which the magnetic field is itself formed must flow from that field to the iron particles, so that they can use it in turn to produce their own magnetic fields. . . In the creative act, the mind and the emotions are aligned in deep inner harmony within the creative field, bringing about lasting transformation (James Varigu in *Creativity*, Synthesis Magazine, June 1978 p. 23; quoted in Lois Robbins, *Waking Up in the Age of Creativity*, Bear and Co., Santa Fe 1985, pp. 156f.).

The limitations of this image, however, striking as it is, is that it suggests that human creative energy is contained within an entropic system. This is not so; see the discussion of entropy on pp. 72ff.

16. Paul Klee, *On Modern Art*, Faber 1966, p. 55.
17. cf. Martin Buber:

Every great culture rests on an original relational incident, on a response to the *Thou* made at its source, on an act of the being made by the spirit. . . If a culture ceases to be centred in the living and continually renewed relational event, then it hardens into the world of *It*, which the glowing deeds of solitary spirits only spasmodically break through (Martin Buber, *I and Thou*, T. & T. Clark 1937, p. 54.).

4   *Art and its Enemies*

1. e. e. cummings, *Selected Poems 1923–58*, Faber 1960, p. 75.

2. Georges Braque, *Notebooks 1917–1955*, Dover Publications, NY 1971, p. 10.)

3. This view of art and its purpose is not of course confined to dictatorships. It can turn up in what might otherwise pass for quite respectable liberal circles. Here is an illuminating example:

> The only way of expressing emotion in the form of art is by finding an 'objective correlative'; in other words a set of objects, a situation, a chain of events which shall be the formula of that particular emotion; such that when the external facts, which must terminate in sensory experience, are given, the emotion is immediately evoked.

How much safer art becomes when its language has been reduced to formulae each of which automatically and predictably elicits its own reaction. The writer here is T. S. Eliot, in his essay on Hamlet (included in T. S. Eliot, *Selected Prose* ed John Hayward, Penguin 1953, p. 102). Not entirely surprisingly Eliot finds Shakespeare's play 'most certainly an artistic failure'.

What is true of the visual arts is also true of verbal language. In George Orwell's *Nineteen Eighty-four* the reduction of all language to a simple authorized form effectively eliminates the freedom to think outside these forms.

> Don't you see that the whole aim of Newspeak is to narrow the range of thought? In the end we shall make thoughtcrime literally impossible, because there will be no words in which to express it. Every concept that can ever be needed will be expressed by exactly one word, with its meaning rigidly defined and all its subsidiary meanings rubbed out and forgotten. . . The Revolution will be complete when the language is perfect (George Orwell, *Nineteen Eighty-four*, Secker and Warburg 1949; Penguin 1970, p. 44.).

4. It would of course be unjust to dismiss all so-called expressionist art (and here I am thinking particularly of the artists of the first three decades of this century whose work is commonly so described) as having nothing to offer but rhetoric. Roger Cardinal in a recent study is at pains to show how such painters as Van Gogh, Kokoschka, Marc and Kandinsky were concerned to express more than a purely private and individual emotion in their work. (See particularly his Chapter III, 'The Spiritual Impulse', pp. 68ff.) Nevertheless it is rare for the typically expressionist artist to rise far above that level of ego-bound feelings that we have seen to be

characteristic of fantasy. Cardinal is generous to the claims of a number of expressionist painters to be in search of a reality beyond the world of appearances: as Franz Marc put it, 'to transcribe the inner mystical structure of the world'. But he also has reservations.

> We should indeed remember that the Expressionist artist is temperamentally drawn to experiences in which the resources of individuality are – somehow – safeguarded. And so, even though he may be tempted by the notion of the self dissolving in ecstatic union with the cosmos, he may equally want to reassert his individuality in face of this excessive act of abandonment (Roger Cardinal, *Expressionism*, Paladin Books 1984, p. 77).

The limitations of the modern European expressionist movement are revealed in the document which was in some ways its most impressive manifesto, Wassily Kandinsky's *Concerning the Spiritual in Art*, Munich 1912, where 'the spiritual' ('das Geistige') is conceived of in terms more appropriately to be described as psychological. His constant reiteration of the part to be played in the work of the artist by 'inner necessity' suggests, once more, a penchant for fantasy rather than an openness to the transcendent.

Cardinal asks the question (of abstract expressionism), 'Is this not an art of autistic sterility, detached from life?' and gives the answer, 'If the Expressionist is authentically in touch with his creative resources, he will . . . arrive at last at a primal site within himself, at a central locus of confident fertility whence spring the truest impulses.' This does seem to concede that Expressionism falls short of that creative experience in which 'the truest impulses' are sensed as having an origin wholly, or at least partially, beyond the artist's own resources. Contrast this view with that of Ben Nicholson, an artist who also reflected deeply on his experience of the creative process, for whom the work of art was something 'more real than life itself'. To him, Expressionism was simply 'beside the point' (M. de Sausmarez (ed), *Ben Nicholson*, Studio International, NY 1969, p. 46).

5. 'In itself it (expressionism) is essentially adequate to express religious meaning directly. . . The rediscovery of the expressive element in art since about 1900 is a decisive event for the relation of religion and the visual arts. It has made religious art again possible' (Paul Tillich, *Theology of Culture*, OUP, NY 1959, pp. 73f.).

A few pages earlier he had written:

Whatever the subject matter which an artist chooses, however strong or weak his artistic form, he cannot help but betray by his style his own ultimate concern, as well as that of his group, and his period. He cannot escape religion even if he rejects religion, for religion is the state of being ultimately concerned. And in every style the ultimate concern of a human group or period is manifest (p. 70).

This seems to imply that the style, any style, that most explicitly expresses what a man's ultimate concern is will be religious. The double sense in which Tillich uses this word 'ultimate' quite undermines the force of the argument. It may indicate the limits of my concern, however narrow; it may on the contrary indicate that my concern transcends all limits.

6. Tolstoy was clear on this.

Since discussions as to why one man likes pears and another prefers meat do not help finding a solution of what is essential in nourishment, so the solution of questions of taste in art (to which the discussions on art involuntarily come) not only does not help to make clear in what this particular human activity which we call art really consists, but renders such elucidation quite impossible until we rid ourselves of a conception which justifies every kind of art at the cost of confusing the whole matter (Leo Tolstoy, *What is Art? and Essays on Art*, OUP 1930, pp. 118f.).

Tolstoy's writings on art are helpful in so far as they reject the idea of beauty, however defined, as the starting point. For him the artist is first of all a communicator. So far so good. Unfortunately, however, he makes no allowance for the imaginative work to be done by the viewer (reader, listener), and so puts upon the creative artist the whole responsibility for seeing that his or her work is not beyond the understanding of the mass of humanity, from whom no corresponding creative effort is demanded. The means of which such communication is to be achieved is repeatedly described by Tolstoy in terms of 'infection' or 'contagion'. He has a valuable perception of the power of art to overcome isolation:

The recipient of a truly artistic impression is so united to the artist that he feels as if the work were his own and not someone else's – as if what it expresses were just what he had long been wishing to express. A real work of art destroys in the consciousness of the recipient the separation between himself and the artist, and not that alone, but also between himself and all whose minds receive this work of art. In this freeing of our personality from its separation and isolation, in this uniting of it with others, lies the chief characteristic and the great attractive force of art. If a man is infected by the author's condition of soul, if he feels this emotion and this union with others, then the object which has effected this is art; but if there be no such infection, if there be not this union with the author and with others who are moved by the same work – then it is not art. And not only is infection a sure sign of art, but the degree of infectiousness is also the sole measure of excellence in art. The stronger the infection the better is the art (ibid., p. 228).

There is, I am sure, no need to point out the unfortunate implications of that last sentence. It is not surprising, after this, to find Tolstoy rejecting a great deal of the art, literature and music of the last century. Even Beethoven's Ninth Symphony is not spared.

7. He continues:

Our present age reveals its disharmony precisely in refusing to believe in the art of today as the expression of its true self. Great artists are those who are sensitive to the destiny of the age in which they live. They are like prophets. If their work survives in the generations that come after, it means that it has been faithful to the deepest feelings of its own age (P. R. Regamey, *Religious Art in the Twentieth Century*, Herder and Herder, NY 1963, pp. 135f.).

8. Wilfred Owen, *Collected Poems*, Chatto and Windus 1931, pp. 31, 55, 37.

9. I hope I have made it clear that each of these elements – imitation, rhetoric and journalism – may have their place in any work of the creative imagination that serves a wider vision. An interesting example is George Segal's 'Abraham and Isaac', origin-ally done for a commission from Kent State University, California, and now at Princeton. A sincere and passionately-felt piece of sculpture, it is intensely realistic (Segal's technique involves making life-casts from living models); it is also unmistakably designed to record a particular protest in commemoration of a particular event in history: the shooting of four students on Kent State University campus on 4 May 1970. (In this it is obviously comparable to Picasso's 'Guernica'.) Segal himself claims that all his sculptures 'talk about the value of a single human being and the value of private

thought and private response' (See Jane Dillenberger's scholarly and persuasive article in Apostolos-Cappadona, op. cit.). I have not seen the original, but I do wonder how far the effectiveness of this work as an authentic comment on a single contemporary episode prevents it escaping the limits imposed by its obvious concern to be topically relevant. It may indeed 'belong to its own time', but if it is also to be timeless some deeper exploration of its theme may be required.

This piece is also interesting as an example of an explicitly religious theme (Abraham's sacrifice of his son Isaac) reinterpreted in purely humanistic terms, to be meaningful to a secularized society in which knowledge of the biblical tradition from which it comes is not necessary for an immediate understanding of what the sculptor is trying to say. Indeed, to anyone familiar with the story of Abraham and the part played in it by this particular event, to give such a title to a work that shows so little regard for the spiritual significance of that story may seem merely offensive.

10. Though no direct parallel is intended, it may be suggestive to compare these three ways in which the imagination can be limited with the three lower levels of scriptural interpretation described in the note 3 to Chapter 3. None are wrong in themselves, but none are by themselves sufficient. A mind that gets stuck at any one of these levels, or becomes obsessed with any of these forms of pseudo-art, will fall short of those creative possibilities that constitute our full humanity.

11. An illuminating example of self-expression only partly transformed by such recollection is Tennyson's *In Memoriam*. It was not until seventeen years after his friend's death that Tennyson began the publication of the poem. The harvest of those long years of waiting was some fine poetry. *In Memoriam* is 'full of quotations', lines and phrases that have passed into the currency of common speech and are still used by thousands who know nothing of their source. Tennyson himself wrote of his poem: 'It is rather the cry of the human race than mine. In the poem an altogether private grief swells out into the thought of, and hope for, the world' (letter quoted in A. W. Robinson, *In Memoriam*, CUP 1901, p. 187). Yet it cannot as a whole be judged a great poem for the simple reason that its writer is still enmeshed in that 'private grief'. There are passages in which he pleads for our sympathy that cannot be read without embarrassment: passages that are still so full of his feelings that there is no room left for ours.

12. It may be interesting to note that the precise equivalent in

Greek of this stripping away is the word *aphaeresis*, used by Pseudo-Dionysius to describe the means by which alone the ascent towards the divine is to be achieved. 'For if God is beyond all that exists, in order to approach him it is necessary to detach oneself from all that is inferior to Him, that is to say, all that which is'. See V. Lossky, *The Mystical Theology of the Eastern Church*, James Clarke 1957, p. 25.

13. Thus Francois Morellet states his 'constant purpose of reducing to a minimum my arbitrary decisions'. So we have a print based on 'an aleatory distribution of 40,000 black and white squares according to the odd and even numbers of a telephone directory'. In transcribing (one cannot call it creating) such random patterns the artist himself has nothing to say. 'The plastic arts must allow the spectator to find in them what he wants, that is to say what he brings to them himself. Works of art are like picnic areas, where one consumes what one takes there oneself' (Exhibition Catalogue, 1975).

Those who cultivate the void (or silence) as an end in itself may care to reflect on this comment of Ruysbroeck's. He is speaking of 'Men who Practise a False Vacancy':

Behold, such folk, by means of a onefold simplification and a natural tendency, are turned in upon the bareness of their own being. . . And because of the naked emptiness which they feel and possess they say that they are without knowledge and without love, and are exempt from the virtues. . . They have unified themselves in a blind and dark vacancy of their own being; and there, they think, they are one with God, and they take this for the Eternal Blessedness (John of Ruysbroeck, 1293–1381, *The Book of Supreme Truth*, Westminster Maryland Christian Classics 1974, pp. 229ff.).

5 Symbol, Sign and Sacrament

1. It is certainly no intention of mine to devalue metaphor, which is an essential element in any living language of mystery. Thus speaking of the richness of the African religious tradition and the need to study the metaphors which express the concepts central to that tradition John Taylor writes: 'Theology is so largely a matter of metaphors that when a few of them recur in many different parts of a continent we should seize upon them as a kind of Rosetta Stone of spiritual communication.' John Taylor, *The Primal Vision*, p. 175.

2. Thus he writes:

Making absolute the dynamic moments of spiritual experience in Christian ontology and metaphysics may become a great false-hood of static, setting itself up against the eternal truth of the dynamic of absolute spiritual life. The dynamic transcription of religious experience must take precedence over the static trans-cription of religious ontology (Nicholas Berdyaev, *The Meaning of the Creative Act*, Gollancz 1955, p. 19).

Compare Daniel Jenkins' observations on the consequences of extreme ecclesiastical conservatism in Eastern Europe. Urging that 'the element of hope must never be outweighed by that of memory in public worship', he continues:

Large churches exist, notably those of the Orthodox East, which have maintained their liturgies and their beliefs largely unchang-ed over many long centuries, and resolutely resist any modi-fication of them. That gives them considerable institutional tenacity but it may also help to create situations where such tenacity becomes essential because they exist in countries where hope has had to find expression chiefly in anti-Christian forms ('Profane Habit and Sacred Usage', in *Theology*, March 1949.)

3. Frank and Dorothy Getlein, *Christianity in Modern Art*, Bruce Publishing Co., Milwaukee 1961, pp. 1, 21.

I have emphasized the impoverishment that its long divorce from the creative arts has brought to religion. The loss has been no less on the other side. When Paul Klee (see above p. 40) laments the lack of a people to support the work (of the Bauhaus) he articulates the sense of desolation that must afflict any poet or artist who sets out to explore reality without the shared symbolic system or mytho-logy that a living tradition can provide. Such a supportive mytho-logy is beyond the power of any individual to create by him – or herself. The poet must therefore take the risk of going naked and unprotected, risking exposure to spiritual forces that may be as destructive as they are creative. In such a situation there can be no assurance that the exploration of this cthonic underground may lead to a recovery of wholeness rather than to total disintegration. Thus Mark Rothko, writing of New York in the 1940s, could indict Western culture as essentially unpractical, because, unlike earlier and more 'primitive' societies, it could no longer provide an accepted language for transcendent experience.

Even the archaic artist, who had an uncanny virtuosity, found it necessary to create a group of intermediaries, monsters, hybrids, gods and demigods. The difference is that, since the archaic artist was living in a more practical society than ours, the urgency for transcendent experience was understood, and given an official status. As a consequence, the human figure and other elements from the familiar world could be combined with, or participate as a whole in, the enactment of the excesses which characterize this improbable hierarchy. With us the disguise must be complete. The familiar identity of things has to be pulverised in order to destroy the finite associations with which our society increasingly enshrouds every aspect of our environment. Without monsters and gods, art cannot enact our drama: art's most profound moments express this frustration (*Possibilities*, New York 1947, p. 84.)

For further discussion of this point see Heidegger's *What are Poets For?* in Heidegger, *Poetry, Language, Thought*; Lynn Ross-Bryant, *Imagination and the Life of the Spirit*, Scholars Press, California 1981, and in particular ch. 7, 'Literature as Mythopoiesis'.

6   Kitsch in Art and Ritual

1. Astonishingly, the word 'Kitsch' does not appear in the Oxford English Dictionary before the Supplement of 1976. There the first record of its use in English is dated 1926. Though its proximate source is clearly German, Professor Egenter, in his classic study *Kitsch und Christenleben* (edited by Nicolete Gray as *The Desecration of Christ*) mentions a suggestion that the word may actually come from the English word 'sketch', 'to describe the inferior artefacts made to please, or take in, the nineteenth century tourist'. Richard Egenter, *The Desecration of Christ*, Burns Oates 1977, p. 14.

2. Here is Thomas Merton on the subject:

The prevalence of bad so-called sacred art everywhere constitutes a really grave spiritual problem, comparable, for example, to the analogous problem of polluted air in some of our big industrial centers. One breathes the bad air, aware only of a slight general discomfort, headache, stinging of the eyes; but in the long run the effect is grave. One looks at the bad art, in church, in pious magazines, in some missals and liturgical books, or so-called 'holy' pictures; one is aware of a vague spiritual uneasiness and distaste. Or perhaps, worse still, one likes the cheap, emotional, immature and even sensual image that is presented. To like bad sacred art, and to feel that one is helped by it in prayer, can be a symptom of real spiritual disorders of which one may be entirely unconscious, and for which perhaps one may have no personal responsibility ('Sacred Art and the Spiritual Life', in Thomas Merton, *Disputed Questions*, Hollis and Carter 1961, p. 155).

For further discussion of these issues see Egenter, op. cit., especially Chapter 5. It may be noted that both these writers are much better at denouncing bad religious art than at suggesting what should be put in its place. Egenter is quite explicit about his intention, as a moral theologian, to 'approach the subject from the standpoint of Christian ethics rather than from the aesthetic standpoint' (p. 14).

3. My concern in this context has been with religious kitsch. For a more general discussion of kitsch see the masterly comments of Milan Kundera in his novel *The Unbearable Lightness of Being*. He is particularly good on its social and political aspects:

> Kitsch is the aesthetic ideal of all politicians and all political parties and movements. Those of us who live in a society where various political tendencies exist side by side and competing influences cancel or limit one another can manage more or less to escape the kitsch inquisition: the individual can preserve his individuality; the artist can create unusual works. But wherever a single political movement corners power, we find ourselves in the realm of totalitarian kitsch. . . . When I say 'totalitarian', what I mean is that everything that infringes on kitsch must be banished for life: every display of individualism (because a deviation from the collective is a spit in the eye of the smiling brotherhood); every doubt (because anyone who starts doubting details will end up by doubting life itself); all irony (because in the realm of kitsch everything must be taken quite seriously); and the mother who abandons her family or the man who prefers men to women, thereby calling into question the holy decree 'Be fruitful and multiply'. . . . In this light, we can regard the Gulag as a septic tank used by

totalitarian kitsch to dispose of its refuse (Faber 1984, pp. 250ff.).

4. Kathleen Raine, 'A Sense of Beauty', in *Resurgence*, No. 114, January 1986.

5. Ben Nicholson in *Unit One*, ed Herbert Read, Cassell 1934, p. 89; quoted in M. de Sausmarez (ed); *Ben Nicholson*, p. 31.

6. Ben Nicholson in J. L. Martin, B. Nicholson and N. Gabo (eds), *Circle*, Faber 1938, p. 75.

7. The point is perhaps worth exploring further, if only because it may help us to get into perspective the invidious distinctions implied by such terms as 'fine art', 'folk art', 'popular culture' etc. No one will surely dispute that there are forms of art, as there are of literature and music, that demand some degree of education for their full appreciation. But let us also recognize that there is 'high kitsch' as well as 'low kitsch', and that the effeteness of the highbrow may be no less corrupting than insensitivity of the lowbrow – probably more so, in fact, since the styles of popular culture are generally deeply influenced by, where they are not directly derived from, the more sophisticated forms of the previous generation. Revitalization may then come from 'below'. It must be admitted, though, that a culture that feels a conscious need to go back to its roots can more easily draw on the outward style and symbolism of the primitive than recapture its spiritual energy. Such an effort is perhaps always a symptom of cultural exhaustion. An illuminating example is the rediscovery by certain European artists in the earlier years of this century of the tribal arts of West Africa. This has been admirably documented by William Rubin in his *Primitivism in Twentieth Century Art*, Museum of Modern Art, NY 1984. It is evident again and again that the power of the originals is notably lacking in the modern derivatives.

7 The Mystery of Creation

1. William James, *The Varieties of Religious Experience*, Longmans Green 1902, pp. 242, 270.

2. A. E. Housman, 'When first my way to fair I took', in *Collected Poems*, Jonathan Cape 1939, p. 142.

3. James, op. cit., p. 508.

4. See K. S. Malevich, *Essays on Art 1915–1933* ed Troels

Anderson, Vol. I, Rapp and Whiting 1969, pp. 188f. For further comments see my article, 'The Apophatic Art of Kasimir Malevich', in *Studia Mystica*, Vol. II, No. 2, 1979.

5. Cf. Nicholas Berdyaev:

Only evolution is determined; creativity derives from nothing which precedes it. Creativity is inexplicable; creativity is the mystery of freedom. . . Those who would deny the possibility of creation out of nothing must inevitably place creativity in a certain determined order and by this very fact must deny the freedom of creativity. In creative freedom there is an inexplicable and mysterious power to create out of nothing, undetermined, adding energy to the existing circulation of energy in the world (Berdyaev, *The Meaning of the Creative Act*, p. 144).

Cf. also Paul Goodman:

The coming of the spirit is new creation. From nothing. In the fields where I have any first-hand acquaintance, literature, social institutions, therapy, the relation of master and apprentice, the conservation of energy is not prima facie; it is far-fetched. Nobody in such fields would think of it. The weight of evidence is that there are continual flashes of creation, order made from nothing, against entropy. There are initiative, invention and insight, and there are routine, falling apart and entropy, but the entropy does not look like the dominant trend. We would not see the passage of the prophetic into the bureaucratic if we were not struck by the prophetic. . . My bias is to deny the theory of conservation (Paul Goodman, *Speaking and Language: Defence of Poetry*, Wildhood House 1973, p. 117).

6. C. E. Montague, *A Writer's Notes*, Penguin 1949, pp. 184f.
7. Cf. William Anderson:

Works of art are storehouses of psychic energy and they transmit this energy according to the quality of attention we bring to them. . . . Every now and then we experience certain works of art so deeply that the memory of them returns again and again to persuade us the energy is not lost but has been transferred to us and stored in the depths of our nature (William Anderson, *Dante the Maker*, Routledge and Kegan Paul 1940, p. 5).

8. Christopher Alexander, *The Timeless Way of Building*, OUP, NY 1979, pp. 19ff.

8 Theology and Childhood

1. In David Wagoner, *Straw for the Fire*, from the Notebooks of Theodore Roethke, University of Washington Press 1980, p. 250.
2. See E. A. Robinson, *The Original Vision*, Seabury Press, NY 1983.
3. Edwin Muir, *Autobiography*, Faber 1938, p. 33.
4. Cf. Barnett Newman:

In our inability to live the life of a creator can be found the meaning of the fall of man. It was a fall from the good, rather than from the abundant, life. And it is precisely here that the artist today is striving for a closer approach to the truth concerning original man than can be claimed by the paleontologist, for it is the poet and the artist who are concerned with the function of original man and who are trying to arrive at his creative state. What is the *raison d'être*, what is the explanation of the seemingly insane drive of man to be painter and poet if it is not an act of defiance against man's fall and an assertion that he return to the Adam of The Garden of Eden? For the artists are the first men (Barnett Newman, 'The first Man was an Artist' in *The Tiger's Eye*, New York, October 1947, No. 1, p. 59).

The contrary view is asserted by Jacques Maritain, for whom all art derives from craft:

Art does not begin with freedom and beauty for beauty's sake. It begins with making instruments for human life, canoes, vases, arrows, necklaces or wall-paintings destined to subject, through magical or non-magical signs, the human environment to the mastery of man. Art must never forget its origins. Man is *Homo faber* and *Homo poeta* together. But in the historical evolution of mankind the *Homo faber* carries on his shoulders the *Homo poeta* (Jacques Maritain, *Creative Intuition in Art and Poetry*, Princeton University Press 1977, p. 45).

5. Wallace Stevens, *Opus Posthumous*, Alfred Knopf, NY 1957, p. 238.

9 Personal Postscript

1. 'The Cardinal's First Tale', in Isak Dinesen, *Last Tales*, Putnam & Co. 1957, pp. 3ff.

2. 'Certum est quia impossibile est', *De Carne Christi*, 5. He would doubtless have appreciated Emily Dickinson's

Impossibility, like wine
Exhilarates the man
Who tastes it: possibility
Is flavorless.
(From *The Complete Poems* ed T. H. Johnson, Faber 1970, p. 838.)

3. A meeting of poets and theologians at the College of preachers in Washington, DC in 1967 produced some illuminating discussion on this question. The poet Denise Levertov commented:

The first thing I wrote down as you began to speak was 'the crisis of myth is the crisis of imagination'. When the imagination fails we cannot walk on the face of the waters, and it does fail. No one but Jesus has so walked. Yet it was His beautiful excess that made Him able. We too could learn with enough passion to walk the lake, to pass through the looking-glass. One of the curious things, reading the papers, is to see that poets in their peculiar ways are believers and the theologians are sceptics (*Parable, Myth and Language* ed Tony Stoneburner, The Church Society for College Work, Cambridge, Mass. 1968, p. 14).

4. 'A, a, a, Domine Deus', in David Jones, *The Sleeping Lord*, Faber 1974, p. 9.
5. Nicholas Wolterstorff, art. cit. in Apostolos-Cappadona, *Art, Creativity and the Sacred*, p. 272.